A Publication of the Egon-Sohmen-Foundation

D0364732

Herbert Giersch (Ed.)
for the Egon-Sohmen-Foundation

Towards a Market Economy
in Central and Eastern Europe

WITHDRAWN

JUN 0 1 2017

Springer-Verlag
Berlin Heidelberg New York
London Paris Tokyo
Hong Kong Barcelona
Budapest

HC
244
.T698
1991

Prof. Dr. Herbert Giersch
Past President
Kiel Institute of World Economics
P. O. Box 4309
W-2300 Kiel 1, FRG

This book was produced with financial support of the Egon-Sohmen-Foundation

ISBN 3-540-53922-0 Springer-Verlag Berlin Heidelberg New York
ISBN 0-387-53922-0 Springer-Verlag New York Berlin Heidelberg

Library of Congress Cataloging-in-Publication Data
Towards a market economy in Central and Eastern Europe / Herbert Giersch, ed. p. cm.
ISBN 0-387-53922-0 (U.S.)
1. Europe, Eastern – Economy policy – 1989– 2. Central Europe-Economic policy. 3. Germany
(West) – Economic policy. I. Giersch, Herbert. HC244.T698 1991 338.943 – dc20 91-13608 CIP

This work is subject to copyright. All rights are reserved, whether the whole or part of the material is
concerned, specifically the rights of translation, reprinting, reuse of illustrations, recitation, broadca-
sting, reproduction on microfilms or in other ways, and storage in data banks. Duplication of this publication or parts thereof is only permitted under the provisions of the German Copyright Law of September 9, 1965, in its current version, and a copyright fee must always be paid.

© Springer-Verlag Berlin Heidelberg 1991
Printed in Germany

42/3140 543210 – Printed on acid-free paper

Preface

In 1990, the countries of Central and Eastern Europe began or accelerated their transition to a market economy. For a newly established foundation in economics—the Egon-Sohmen-Foundation, which had no previous commitments—this was the one subject that appeared to deserve first priority in planning a series of conferences.

A small number of experts from ex-socialist countries and the USSR were invited to discuss in an intimate atmosphere their common or special problems among each other and with the organizers and some other participants.

Apart from the peculiarities of individual countries that were stressed by participants, several major questions came up in the initial discussion as well as in the final debate:

(i)   Is the transition process to a market economy irreversible?

(ii)   What major steps could and should be taken to reach and pass the point of no return?

(iii)   What can be learned from the experience of postwar economic reform in West Germany?

(iv)   If macroeconomic stability is a precondition, what is the role of privatization, deregulation and trade liberalization?

(v)   If the issue of gradualism versus shock therapy is ill conceived, what is the optimal sequence of steps in privatization, deregulation, liberalization and currency convertibility? Is convertibility on capital account an essential precondition for other steps or must it be postponed until the very end of the transition process?

(vi)   How quickly can privatization be achieved? And by which method? How quickly will an entrepreneurial spirit and an efficient business culture develop from dispersed and private ownership and unregulated or regulated markets with or without competition from abroad?

(vii) Is the USSR really a special case and, if so, in what respects and for what fundamental reasons?

(viii) How long in the transition period will the initial phase of disorder, chaos and decline last and what improvement in productivity, employment and living standards can be expected in the subsequent ten year period?

(ix) How important would it be to offer a type of "Marshall Plan" in the form of aid from government to government?

(x) If such aid is envisaged, what preconditions should be established to make it successful and what strings should be attached so that public aid can become the pacemaker for private capital flows?

No precise answers, of course, emerged in the discussion, since no one can foresee the future. The debate thus will go on, even for decades, long after the historical epoch of transition has been completed, say in the course of the 1990s.

We appreciate that the authors let us publish the papers in the form of a book though they were aware that in the meantime their views and their assessment of the situation might not remain unaltered under the impact of a fast and dramatic change in circumstances. They well understood that we all find ourselves in a process of learning that will be most efficient if it takes place in the context of an open multilateral system of trade in ideas.

But we deliberately made no preparations for summarizing the discussion, as the exchange of views during the conference was to be as unconstrained as possible. Instead, we included three complementary papers.

Holger Schmieding gave invaluable help in establishing the program, and Friedrich Schmidt-Bleek generously offered us the hospitality of the International Institute for Applied Systems Analysis (IIASA) in Laxenburg, Austria, where the conference took place on 22-23 May 1990. Simone Ferling deserves credit for joyfully editing the manuscript.

The Egon-Sohmen-Foundation owes its existence to Dr. Helmut Sohmen of Hong Kong who established it in memory of his late brother, who was an outstanding economist well known in North America as well as in Central Europe. Born in Linz, Austria, in 1930, Egon Sohmen taught at MIT and Yale and in Minnesota and held chairs as a full professor at the Universities of Saarbrücken and Heidelberg, where he died at the early age of 46. His areas of interest in which he became prominent include competition and allocation theory and international economics. He was a great champion of economic freedom and strongly believed in the superiority of the market system over central planning. There is no doubt that he would have been an active intellectual supporter of the transition to a market economy in Central and Eastern Europe. The first conference of the foundation established in his name would have been close to his heart.

Herbert Giersch

Contents

Herbert Giersch

Some General Lessons from West Germany's Postwar Experiences

West Germany is widely acclaimed for having produced an economic "miracle" in the wake of the 1948 currency reform and the parallel decontrol of prices. A miracle it was indeed. It came as a surprise to everybody, except perhaps some notorious optimists. This is already part of the explanation. Germany's economic performance would have been much less impressive had the fast productivity advance been fully anticipated at the wage bargaining table. Profits and profit expectations would have been lower, and much less business investment would have come forth. The structural (classical) unemployment, which was related to an inadequate capital stock (capital shortage unemployment), would have persisted for a longer time, and the tensions between the indigenous population and the immigrants from the eastern part of the former "Reich" (refugees and so-called expellees) could well have led to social unrest. In this respect, one can say that positive surprises produced positive suprises. A virtuous circle developed. One cannot say how important this "pure miracle" was. But it is unlikely to repeat itself elsewhere, not even in East Germany. The main reason is that it has been cited often enough to unduly raise hopes for a repetition, and the excessive expectations that these hopes are likely to develop will prevent a wage lag from emerging. And wage moderation is the key element in a process of fast growth.

Apart from moderate expectations, West Germany's rapid postwar recovery was due to hard work. In the late 1950s, when Austria paralleled Germany's remarkable performance, people joked that the true miracle occurred in Austria because the Germans were known to be hard workers.

This work ethic was partly rooted in tradition. To some important part, it was probably also a result of the desperate postwar living conditions in Germany. Most people entertained the belief that only self-help would permit them to regain the living standard they had already enjoyed before the war. Catching-up with one's own past achievements (reconstruction) was also seen as a realistic target. It is a less ambitious goal, and potentially less frustrating, than the goal of catching-up with one's neighbors, i.e., closing a geographical gap as it then existed vis-à-vis North America or as it now exists between East and West Germany or between Eastern and Western Europe. The lesson is this: Where living standards have fallen, as in Poland, the initial recovery, the catching-up with the past, can be quick; this phase is likely to show more growth than can be expected during the initial phase in countries such as Czechoslovakia which suffered no such setback.

Human capital is more important than physical capital. Together with geography, human capital can well determine a country's long-run potential for growth. In 1948, West Germany had an ample supply of human capital despite the losses inflicted by war. Many among the members of the former military class found their way into business, to become successful entrepreneurs. Immigrants from the Eastern provinces (refugees) also played an important role. In order to assess their importance one has to recognize a persistent tendency: ever since the industrialization of the Rhine-Ruhr valley there was a decline of incomes from the West to the East—with the exception of Berlin—due to transportation costs. The prospect of high incomes in the West brought about an inflow of people from the East, including Poland. After 1945, this change occurred as a shock rather than a continuous flow. It laid the demographical ground for a sudden rise in West Germany's growth potential.

As to the future, one can say that the role of the growth center for Central and Eastern Europe will continue to be played by the regions close to the estuary of the Rhine and the Rhine valley. Therefore, the tendency for incomes to decline towards Eastern Europe will persist in the foreseeable future as long as distance and transportation costs matter. These costs can be brought down by infrastructure investments: they would raise the long run income potential in Eastern Europe. But in the short run, geography is certainly not the limiting factor there.

West Germany quickly attained its long-run potential for income in part because of its proximity to the centers of Western civilization. The process of catching-up was accompanied by internal migration. The refugees and expellees from the East who were initially allocated to the agricultural regions quickly moved to the centers of economic activity, where they found jobs and discovered entrepreneurial opportunities. It is doubtful whether such mobility can be taken for granted in present-day Eastern Europe, but it may well be that the existing degree of urbanization (and industrialization) offers a sufficient growth potential for many years to come and that, therefore, a lack of internal mobility need not turn out to be a limiting factor for growth.

Emigration, though, is a danger. It did not play any role at all in West Germany after 1945. There was hardly any brain drain; and the excess supply of labor relative to capital made Germany a low wage country, at least in the early years of reconstruction. Mention must also be made of an institutional weakness of labor unions in the early years. High profits ploughed back into job-creating investments enhanced employment opportunities. These opportunities contributed to limiting emigration when other countries were again prepared to accept immigrants from Germany. Conditions in present-day Eastern Europe may be less favorable. The GDR is a case in point. It obtained its political freedom under the threat of "exit and voice," with mass exit, or the mere threat of it, leading to economic union with West Germany. For the future, the problem is to find a level and a structure of wages that is in tune with the low level of productivity but gives enough incentives for highly skilled workers to stay in the region instead of looking for a job in West Germany. The solution lies in a wage structure which is very much differentiated: high pay for mobile, skilled workers and entrepreneurs, very low pay for unskilled workers, who are likely to be immobile as they would hardly find a job in West Germany. In more general terms, one of the most important conditions for the catching-up of an open economy is the acceptance by the populace of a minimum degree of income inequality to allow not only for high profits from business investment but also for high returns on human capital and entrepreneurship. Will people in the ex-socialist countries, with their egalitarian tradition, be capable of intuitively understanding this necessity?

The formation of new human capital was no problem in postwar Germany. The universities were quickly restored, and casual observation confirms the widespread view amongst professors that the student cohorts of the immediate postwar period were eager to recoup whatever time they had lost because of the war. Training on the job was widespread in industry, and for young workers and even ex-soldiers the dual system of professional schooling and apprenticeships proved to be efficient. The present author cannot judge whether Eastern Europe will have bottlenecks in the field of professional education. East Germany certainly suffers from great shortfalls in higher education in economics and the humanities and may also lack an adequate level and structure of skills, particularly for the service sector. Should the situation be similar in other parts of Eastern Europe, it will be more difficult for them to correct than for East Germany, which can rely on Western help to come from the German language area.

For decades, West Germany has received praise and criticism for the high savings rate of its population. The same holds for the peoples of Japan and the Asian NICs, much in contrast to the low rates of household savings in North America and South America. We do not know exactly why savings rates differ, but it is plausible to assume for the present-day (non-Keynesian) world that a high propensity to save is almost a guarantee of fast long-term growth: people who care for their future needs are also on the watch for any future income opportunities arising from the growth of knowledge. One is tempted to allude to the notion of a capitalist spirit, though this might imply in the present context that North America lacks an essential feature of capitalism. Nevertheless, the U.S. of today can afford now what Germany after 1945 could not afford and what the ex-socialist countries of Eastern Europe cannot afford either.

Many observers contend that Marshall Plan aid permitted a resource inflow that West Germany would not have obtained otherwise. This is an exaggeration. The same foresight that enlightened U.S. government officials had about the prospects of European recovery in 1949 would otherwise have inspired the World Bank and other lending institutions to step in—perhaps with some delay and perhaps demanding somewhat higher interest rates. But Germany and Europe had the absorptive capacity and could have easily earned whatever interest the market would have requested. This judgement may rest on the benefit of hindsight, but such hindsight has to be taken into account when we draw lessons for the future and for Eastern Europe. What Marshall Plan aid accomplished over and above a comparable private lending scheme was to convince the politicians in the recipient countries that there should be European economic cooperation for trade liberalization and an organization to press for it (the OEEC).

Except for a short period in the wake of the Korean boom, West Germany never had an alarming deficit in its current account balance. Most of the time, even during the reconstruction period, it was a capital exporter, largely due to its households' and businesses' high propensity to save. Initially these capital exports served to finance direct investment for export promotion.

Part of the miraculous output growth in the period before 1950 must be ascribed to the extraordinarily high productivity of the investment needed to repair the capital stock and to widen bottlenecks in the capacity structure, including the transport system. It was as if the capital stock had been much less destroyed during the war, or as if spare capacity had just waited to be made accessible. Such a "repair" effect in the ex-socialist countries is unlikely to occur. But there must be inherent wastes from the misallocation of investment resources that could be reduced in a short time under the pressure of competition and under the guidance of relative prices reflecting relative securities. Instead of what we may call a "repair miracle" after destruction in war, there could perhaps occur a "reallocation miracle" after a painful period of restructuring.

A precondition for such a production miracle was and seems to be the decontrol of prices and the removal of central planning and administration. In West Germany, this was largely accomplished in connection with the currency reform.[1] It made the currency reform successful, but could have been carried out without it; the proviso is that the money supply in the old currency had had to be strictly controlled. The actual combination of the two reforms in the West German case can easily lead to the wrong conclusion that the currency reform deserves all the praise and that a currency reform in Eastern Europe, or a monetary union in the case of East Germany, is almost all that is needed. Stable money is important, but it must be freely convertible into all kinds of goods and services—present ones and future ones. In other words, money has to be stable in a market with freely flexible prices for all assets. And for a production miracle to take place, markets must be competitive and, therefore, widely open for upstarts as well as for foreign suppliers.

Against this background, the 1948 reforms in West Germany had several shortcomings:[2] (i) Not all price controls were lifted immediately. Exempted from decontrol were basic foodstuffs and raw materials, housing rents, and public services. To the extent that decontrol had reduced the real incomes of the poor below the subsistence level, direct income subsidies would have been more appropriate. (ii) While a unified exchange rate was established in 1948, foreign trade and payments remained under tight control until 1950. (iii) The capital market was not liberalized, so

---

[1] For details see the article by Schmieding in this volume.

[2] See also the article by Schmieding in this volume.

that firms had to rely on retained profits for investment to a large extent.

What was the reason for maintaining these controls? Apart from vested interests inside the German control bureaucracy and apart from international political misconceptions about the future role of raw materials in international power politics, the basic reason was a widespread pessimism about supply elasticities: the situation would worsen before it could improve. Indeed, the J-curve effect was intuitively well understood. This holds for all markets, including the balance of payments. What can be learned from this, with the benefit of hindsight, is that fears of low supply elasticities are not warranted except in the short run; they should be laid to rest when it comes to making fundamental decisions. Postponement of reform does not help. After the event, the patient will be proud and happy to have dared to have the operation (the early lifting of controls or the timely correction of an unrealistic exchange rate); and some years afterwards, people will appreciate the time they gained for recovery and growth. The switch from a system of control to a system of free markets surely requires tremendous political courage. But equally high can be the political gains in the medium run. At the polls, the Germans fully appreciated what they owed to Erhard.

It took Ludwig Erhard ten years to work for full currency convertibility on capital account. The goal could have been reached much earlier, say, in 1954, shortly after the conclusion of the London Debt Agreement. The damage resulting from the postponement was probably small, thanks to the high domestic savings rate. It would have been much larger had Germany had to rely on capital imports. This should be remembered in discussions about the pros and cons of an early move to full currency convertibility in

Eastern Europe. East Germany obtained full convertibily in July 1990 when it became part of the official D-Mark area.

Trade liberalization was delayed under the impact of the postwar "dollar shortage" which is just another name for the overvaluation of most other currencies, including the D-Mark. Given this overvaluation, Marshall Plan aid helped. But foreign aid also made a devaluation less necessary. A more realistic exchange rate would have had the advantage of raising the profitability of investment in the export sector and in the import substitution sector, surely at the expense of investment in the domestic sector. The integration of the West German economy into the world economy could have been faster. Exploiting, right from the start, the benefits of the international division of labor is likely to offer a payoff in terms of a lower (incremental) capital/output ratio. With given investment—and perhaps with additional capital imports—postwar growth in Germany could have been even more miraculous. This view is confirmed by the experience that the small open economies in Asia subsequently made when they embarked upon an export-oriented growth strategy.

Trade liberalization, later followed by the formation of the EEC customs union, must also be seen as a method of inviting foreign competitive pressures to suppress monopolistic tendencies. The fact that foreign exporters are most eager to enter the home market does not mean that they are the only beneficiaries. They share the benefits with domestic consumers. And a government and central bank responsible for price level stability must realize that import competition is their ally in preventing cost push inflation during a cyclical upswing. Such considerations played a role in German policy-making when Erhard successfully pressed for unilaterally cutting tariffs on imports from EEC countries, ahead of the schedule laid down in the Treaty of Rome. Import liberalization also made it less harmful (than it would have been otherwise) that the competition law establishing the Cartel Office did not pass legislature before 1957. The lesson for Eastern Europe seems to be clear: import liberalization must be part of the reform package.

West Germany was lucky to have inherited from the past a structure of industrial production well suited to a growing world demand. An export mix strongly biased in favor of machinery and equipment and sophisticated durable consumer goods—with a high income elasticity of demand—permitted improvements in the terms of trade. It were these terms-of-trade improvements that showed up in surprisingly high productivity gains, i.e., gains which could not be anticipated in collective wage bargaining. In this sense, the export performance was crucial for profits and hence also for the investment and growth miracle.

The lesson for East European countries is clear. They must dare to liberalize imports not only to lower costs in the import substitution sector but also to shift resources into the export sector. The whole process of subjecting domestic producers to international competition should be accompanied by efforts to transfer personnel from purchasing departments to sales departments. Marketing should, of course, include activities that are intended to discover market niches in Western countries. A flexible exchange rate supported by a tight monetary policy should make all this easier than it was for Germany in the early days after the 1948 currency reform, when the exchange rate was fixed and overvalued.

The ideal is an exchange rate that appears to be undervalued—defined in terms of the production costs of standardized manufactured products. Such an exchange rate attracts foreign investors; they find the new location well suited for serving their old customers at home. The inflow of foreign capital goods for such investment surely creates an import surplus on current account, i. e., a current account deficit, but these additional imports are complementary to domestic production. Instead of destroying jobs in the import substitution sector, as many may think, they create jobs for additional exports and hence for additional imports. They thus accelerate the growth of external trade. The current account deficit involved should not be viewed as a sign of weakness—i. e., as "living beyond one's means." In this case, it obviously is the result of strength—of investing beyond one's savings. This strength will be reflected in a fast rate of increase of exports, since foreign firms now serve their former home market increasingly from their new locus of production.

The German balance-of-payments crisis of 1950 was initially interpreted as a disastrous event. But it soon became clear that the deficit was due not to overspending by domestic households but to business investment needed for widening production bottlenecks and for building up raw material stocks parallel to quickly expanding production levels. In such a case, it is easy to remove the deficit; it can be done by putting on the monetary brakes. As exports are rising fast, a mere slowdown of business imports is sufficient; no lowering of the standard of living is at stake. The lesson from this is important: current account deficits are a reflection of capital imports; but only in case that the imported capital is used for consumption, private or government, is the current account deficit a symptom of weakness. Under flexible exchange rates, judgement will be passed by the exchange market. In the case of a deficit arising from excess consumption, the currency will devalue (in real terms) in order to bring about a shift of resources from the domestic sector to the export sector and the import substitution sector. But if the deficit is a sound one, reflecting imports for additional investment, its emergence may go along with an appreciation that arises from the attempts of foreign business to acquire domestic resources complementary to the resources they bring into the country.

West Germany, after a defeat in war, had no reservations against full economic integration into the international economy. Its leading economists were internationally minded and even cosmopolitan by conviction or as a reaction to the excesses of previous policies aimed at autarchy. The idea of European economic integration became a publicly accepted substitute for patriotism. Businessmen tended to be outward-looking, and professional success often depended on experiences gained abroad. Internationalization thus contributed to the reemergence of a capitalist spirit. All this will happen in the ex-socialist countries, but it is likely to take more time than it did in West Germany.

The internationalization of West Germany proceeded faster than most people at home or abroad had expected or feared. When after the German balance-of-payments crisis the present author had to make a rough forecast of German export growth during the next decade, he made two assumptions: (i) The German export sector in relation to GNP would become as large as the export sector in Britain, and (ii) the economy would grow by about seven percent per year to double its size in ten years. Because of the first assumption exports were envisaged to almost explode. This result was held to be untenable and it was thought it would provoke counterproductive repercussions in international circles. Therefore, the author had to withdraw the paper. In actual fact, German exports in 1960 turned out to be six times as high as in 1950. Moreover, during this period, productivity in the international sector of the German economy ("tradables") grew more than twice as fast as in the domestic sector ("nontradables").

Most East European countries can be presumed to have similar prospects in the years to come. The argument that existing markets, or the world economy, offer little scope for newcomers has often been made and has equally as often been disproved. But one has to recognize: the world market is dominated by competition, and this includes a search process that is not and cannot be successful in each and every case of entrepreneurial action.

With some exception, West Germany, in its postwar growth process, has hardly missed an opportunity to exploit the productivity potential of the international division of labor. The exceptions are in the areas of agriculture, coal and steel, shipbuilding, textiles and clothing. This high level of specialization is in contrast to what we observe in East European economies. They suffer from underspecialization, even within the domestic sector. It is worthwhile to look at the deeper causes.

Specialization means concentrating on those products and activities that promise the highest return relative to their costs, so that the return on the capital invested attains the highest possible level. The maximization of profits per unit of capital requires that there are capitalists to press for it. These capitalists hire and fire the managers, who may turn out to be innovative entrepreneurs with good luck or unhappy losers and perhaps mere scapegoats. The role of the capitalist is essential, whether the functions are performed by an investment trust, a bank, a multitude of shareholders or even a public authority. Government institutions fulfill the capitalist's function badly because they exert political influence in the choice of managers and create moral hazard problems by being able to cover losses out of taxpayers' money.

When West Germany became a market economy in 1948, it happened after an interval of a mere dozen years of control compared to a period of 40 or even more than 70 years of socialism in present-day Eastern Europe. More important perhaps is that the pre-1948 system was not socialism but controlled capitalism. Private property, though impaired, had survived throughout the whole Nazi rule; the system of property rights had remained essentially intact; and the capitalist spirit was still alive. Deconcentration had to be performed by the Allied authorities; but privatization was not a point on the agenda for reconstruction and recovery. This is a big difference. It makes the transition towards a true market economy in Eastern Europe much more difficult. [3]

The smooth functioning of markets strongly depends upon a system of rules embedded in private law and built upon mutual trust among people who have acquired a reputation for trustworthiness. Trustworthiness is a private asset. A contract partner wanting to stay in business is strongly interested in implementing a contract. Otherwise, he or she might loose the advantage of lower transaction and credit costs. But the existence of a business community with well-established ethical rules of behavior is also an asset for society. As a conservative element, it can degenerate and lead to conformism and implicit cartels. Therefore, it must be combined with openness towards newcomers and entrepreneurship. For this, liberalization and export orientation are important. On the other hand,

---

[3] See also the article by Schmieding in this volume.

entrepreneurship without a conservative background may turn out to be mere "adventurism." Postwar West Germany can be said to have quickly reestablished or developed a liberal-conservative business culture. Eastern Europe, after forty years of central planning and autarchy, may need a much longer time to attain a similar standard. Formal education can help, but the main task will have to be accomplished in a process of learning by doing. In this process, errors and acts of misbehavior should be widely publicized. But they should not not be blamed on the system of free markets. Countries and regions in closer contact with, and with better access to, Western markets will be under stronger pressure and will, therefore, have to move more quickly along the learning curve.

Property rights is a similar issue. After 1945, West Germany faced no difficulties in achieving a reputation as a country with an impeccable system of private property rights. It is true that the constitution (the "Basic Law") contains a clause constraining property rights by subjugating them to the general welfare, but, so far, this has had no significant negative implication for saving and investment and for international capital movements. Germany's attractiveness on the world capital market continues to be high even though the country is not one of the frontrunners in the recent international competition for deregulation, liberalization, privatization, and lower business taxes. East European countries, both as debtors and as locations for direct foreign investment, will find it impossible, at least in the foreseeable future, to reach Western standards unless they move at a revolutionary speed in this direction. The task seems to be enormous. Consider only the privatization of socialized property and the compensation of former owners. This alone may require several decades unless it is proceeding at a revolutionary speed, much faster than it was considered necessary in West Germany in the recent past.

Without a massive privatization scheme, East European countries will not be able to build up efficient capital markets. Without well organized capital markets the flow of savings into domestic investment will be severely hampered by high transaction costs or by distorting impediments. Moreover, an anonymous capital market is indispensable for attracting investible funds from abroad. After the war, West Germany had a fairly well-functioning system of private and public banks, including savings banks and banks in the form of cooperatives, which were able to take care of agriculture, crafts and small business. Large banks traditionally give loans to big business. They also hold shares of large firms, so that they exert a strong influence on the appointment of managers. Fears that there was too much power vested in the hands of bank managers, that competition among banks was too weak and that financial services in Germany were too expensive have certainly had their justification. In the early years, of course, they were more founded than they are now after German capital markets have become fully integrated into a worldwide system of financial services. But the task of narrowing the gap between the interest paid by investors and the interest earned by savers still remains to be performed by increasing competition (deregulation).

A market system fully developed to permit firms and individuals to exhaust the potential for the division of labor offers a wide scope for productive intermediaries. This is why in advanced market economies the modern service sector has grown rapidly—initially at the expense of agricultural employment and, after certain income levels have been reached, at the expense of industry. In its growth process, West Germany had an increasing share of industry (manufacturing) until 1970. Only thereafter did services grow at the expense of hardware production: it happened later than in other countries and at a higher level of incomes. For this anomaly, there are various explanations. One is geography: the Rhine river continues to be an important locational factor for the chemical industry; and the Ruhr valley remains the industrial basin for steel and steel-intensive manufacturing. Another explanation lies in export-led growth; it took place with heavy emphasis on the traditional lines of manufacturing, due to the undervaluation vis-à-vis the dollar of the German currency in the 1960s. The issue has not been settled, however.

Similarly uncertain is the answer to the parallel question whether West Germany would have fared better had its production and employment structure changed earlier in favor of services, perhaps at the expense of such mature industries as mass steel production, shipbuilding, textile and clothing, industries that became problem industries in the 1970s. Services could well have absorbed the resources released by industry if they had been less constrained by government regulation. The lesson for East European countries is that we just cannot know what the optimal structure is and which economic activities deserve promotion—necessarily at the expense of others. Surely, industry is not inherently more productive than services as some may think, e.g., politicians or Marxists or laymen. Nor should one conclude from the rapid progress of productive services in advanced capitalist countries that they deserve promotion. The only knowledge we can rely on is that growth requires structural change, that governments and even research institutes can only make pattern predictions, and that hypotheses concerning the productivity of specific activities must be subjected to the profitability test of the market. But the market must be left free—without protective subsidies and without barriers to entry. Otherwise, the findings of market participants in their search process will be distorted. And the market that matters is not smaller than the world market. For this reason, the tasks of privatization, deregulation and liberalization have to be accomplished together, almost simultaneously.

West Germany never had an unfettered, free economy. It therefore produced less growth than would have been possible had people enjoyed and exploited unconstrained life opportunities. The constraints we are criticizing do not include redistributive taxes for supporting those who are poor for reasons they cannot remove. We may also consider compulsory health insurance and the pension system as elements of a Social Market Economy. What has restrained economic growth, however, is wasteful subsidies, the corresponding taxes needed to finance them, and regulations to protect the incomes of insiders, including the employees of socialized industries such as the loss-making railway system and traditional postal services. It proves very difficult to dismantle all these regulations and to cut government support in a democracy in ordinary circumstances. Eastern Europe should, therefore, not imitate or even copy West Germany or Western Europe wherever the market system suffers from government-induced sclerosis.

The growth of government is a drag on economic growth for various reasons. High taxes depress society's motivation level, while high subsidies and other support measures reduce the need for self-help activities. Moreover, government regulations tend to close the market and to weaken competition. Political parties competing for government power in a democratic setting invite pressure from small but well organized interest groups that succeed in demonstrating how desperately they need help or how much they would gain—of course, to the benefit of society and at negligeable cost to the average voter—if they received protection in direct or indirect form. In 1948, West Germany started with a small government sector and a low level of protective regulations due to defeat in war and the breakdown or dismantling of old government institutions. However, the government contributed to capital formation by achieving budget surpluses for a number of years. All this changed for the worse, notably in the interventionist 1970s. Government absorption, including social security, was still less than one third before 1960 and is now close to one half despite strong political efforts, in the 1980s, to reduce the size of government relative to GNP. East European countries will find it extremely difficult to cut down their huge government sectors. Public sector employees do not only draw salaries; they also have a quite natural tendency to show their effectiveness by demanding and spending additional funds. This danger will be particularly great in periods of transition when tight adminstrative and fiscal controls are loosened. Why should regulators be interested in deregulation? Why should planning administrators work hard for privatization?

West Germany never really suffered from fiscal chaos, though there were periods when public spending appeared to be rather uncontrolled in comparison to the fiscal austerity preceeding them. In the last analysis, the authority to bring pressure to bear on the central government was the Bundesbank. Being independent and devoted to the objective of maintaining price level stability, the Bundesbank was able, most of the time, to oppose demands for a more expansive monetary policy. It thus forced the government to borrow at relatively high interest rates on the open capital market. Over and above this, the Bundesbank was even in a position to tighten its policy when the growth of government debt threatened to worsen the country's external account and to weaken the D-Mark in foreign exchange markets. In this respect, as in others, an informed public, sensitive to the issues of external and internal stability, was the Bundesbank's best ally.

In less favorable circumstances, it will be advisable to stipulate in the country's constitution that the central bank is solely responsible for maintaining the value of legal tender under conditions of full convertibility and that the fiscal authorities' power to borrow—even on the open capital market—must be strictly limited to financing investments that promise to be sufficiently productive to earn the market rate of interest.

If the central bank is independent of government, how can it be controlled? The answer is: by competition with other central banks and other issuers of money. The preconditions of such open competition are (i) full convertibility on capital account as well as on trade account, and (ii) the permission for domestic citizens to use in contracts whatever currency they consider to be the best unit of account. As already indicated, West Germany did not introduce full convertibility before 1958 (although it could have done so after 1953), mainly due to the resistance of the persons operating the system of foreign exchange control. However, West Germany never lifted the stipulation that the D-Mark was to be the only legal tender. This latter provision played an important role after the 1973 oil shock, when even the Bundesbank pursued a policy of accomodation and economists increasingly called for the issue of index-linked bonds as a hedge against inflation. The Bundesbank, of course, defended its legal monopoly position within the German currency area. The arguments used are the same as those put forward against a parallel currency: competition prevents the monopolist from controlling the market. The lesson to be learned from this is simple: independence will not be enough, and competition must be expressly permitted to operate and, if necessary, invited to emerge. Index-linked government bonds would at least be a control device. The difference in interest rates—compared to normal bonds—would clearly indicate the public's inflation expectations, and the central bank will at least know by how much it is likely to miss the target of price level stability.

Many observers may wonder how these statements can be presented as lessons from West Germany's experience with its independent central bank. This is certainly a good question. But, and after all, the marvellous D-Mark, in its short history of four decades, lost not less than two thirds of its initial value.

Holger Schmieding

West Germany's Economic Reforms of 1948:
The Lessons for Central and Eastern Europe Today

In June 1948, West Germany took the great leap from central planning to more or less free markets, a step which initiated a growth spurt that became known as the "Wirtschaftswunder," the German economic miracle. Recently, West Germany's liberal reforms have been cited frequently as an example for the Central and East European countries wanting to transform their Soviet-type economies[1] into market economies. The purpose of the following text is to draw some tentative conclusions from the West German experience for the ex-socialist countries today. In order to do so, the economic situation in West Germany before the reforms, the reforms themselves and their impact will be analyzed in the first two sections, while section three is devoted to the lessons for Central and Eastern Europe.

I. 1945–48: West Germany's Postwar Misery

Since 1936, the Nazis had converted the still predominantly capitalist German economy into a centrally administered system geared towards the needs of the totalitarian state. The main pillars of the Nazi economic legislation had been the fixing of prices, wages and rents at their levels of autumn 1936, the rationing of consumer

---

[1] This term was coined by Winiecki [1988].

goods and foodstuffs, the central allocation of labor and raw materials, a system of compulsory delivery quotas for farmers, and a tight regulation of housing. During the war, the economic system resting on these pillars had reasonably well served its purpose of extracting savings for the rapid build-up of the armaments industry. After the war, the Allies took over this system of directing the economy. Competent central administration might have engineered a substantial recovery, at least for some time, provided it could have gathered adequate information about the resources available, the damages to be repaired and the required structural changes. Yet after the breakdown of the previous administration, the collapse of communications and transportation and the thoroughgoing postwar disruptions of the pattern of production, this was clearly not feasible. Furthermore, the fragmentation of the Reich as well as the gradual build-up of new German authorities, reaching from the local level upwards to the states ("Länder") and the zones, implied that a totally different system of planning had to be erected, a system that could not rely on the previous institutions.

On the microeconomic level, the rigid structure of relative prices did not reflect the postwar scarcities, which differed markedly from prewar conditions. Therefore, price signals could not steer resources into the most productive uses, not even in those cases where the administrative system had left sufficient room for individual initiative. Leaving aside some minor adjustments of the price structure, only the prices for "new" goods were flexible in the sense that, when these goods were introduced, their prices could be determined on the basis of what the authorities accepted as current costs. While there were no adequate economic incentives to spur the production of bottleneck commodities like fertilizers and coal-mining equipment, firms could fare comparatively well by securing attractive prices for luxurious or semiluxurious commodities that had not been available before the war and for which prices had therefore not been fixed previously. Naturally, a flood of such "new" goods as fancy and innovative ash trays, lamps, dolls and chandeliers poured forth.[2] Thus, in the midst of postwar misery, West Germany turned into a "hair-oil, ash-tray, herb-tea economy."[3]

In the macroeconomic domain, the frozen price level did not stand in any realistic relation to the current money supply. After 1932, a ruthlessly expansionary monetary policy had created an inflationary pressure that could not be held in check until the price freeze of 1936. On top of this, the financing of the war through the printing press pushed up the money supply roughly tenfold,[4] whereas by the end of the war, industrial production dropped to about a quarter of what it had been before. With more money chasing fewer goods at fixed prices, Germany found itself in a state of "repressed inflation."[5] The official money lost its value not via rising prices (open inflation) but via a spreading reluctance to accept this money as a medium of exchange.

---

[2] See Balabkins [1964], p. 161.

[3] See Röpke [1951], p. 271. Between mid-1946 and mid-1948, the glass and ceramics industries and the musical instruments and toys industries were by far the most rapidly growing sectors of the West German economy, with employment increasing by 113.5 and 108.4 percent, respectively, about five times as fast as overall employment. Ehret [1959], p. 65; the numbers refer to the Bizonal area only.

[4] For exact figures on circulation, see Buchheim [1988], p. 199.

[5] Röpke [1947], p. 57.

Due to the almost complete repudiation of the official currency, cigarettes replaced the Reichsmark as the standard means of deferred payments and short-term store of value in day-to-day transactions.[6] Even more importantly, firms and individuals resorted to illegal bilateral barter and to complicated compensation deals, often involving arduously worked out chains of bilateral trade to finally get hold of scarce inputs. Both the need to have a sufficient supply of commodities at hand for eventual bartering and the general flight into physical assets as the only reliable stores of value ("Flucht in die Sachwerte") resulted in a large scale hoarding of raw materials and semifinished products.[7]

To sum up, the peculiar combination of an unreliable and ineffective administrative allocation of resources, of illegal markets and of excess liquidity in face of rigidly fixed prices gave rise to widespread inefficient self-production, to very high transaction costs and to a very unfavorable ratio of stocks to output in an economy desparately short of raw materials. Neither sound money nor flexible relative prices were available as the means for coordinating the complex division of labor which is the hallmark of a modern economy. Eventually, as the administrations increasingly lost their grip on the economy, only about half of the output was available through legal channels. The rest was hoarded or used for nominally illegal but widely tolerated compensation deals and for black market transactions.[8]

---

[6]   See Wallich [1955], p. 65.

[7]   See Buchheim [1988], p. 195.

[8]   See Balabkins [1964], p. 147.

As to the macroeconomic performance, the postwar misery showed up in a run-down of the capital stock and a low level of production. In principle, the partial and unevenly distributed destruction of the capital stock should have made investments highly profitable both in repairing existing and installing new equipment for widening bottlenecks. Instead, investment dropped even by a larger percentage than overall production.[9] Three years after the war, the capital stock was 21 percent below its peak level of 1944 and 7.4 percent below its 1945 level, with the machines being on average older than before.[10] And although some progress was made in comparison with the collapse at the end of the war, industrial production between 1945 and early 1948 limped at around one third of its 1938 level. Furthermore, food output fell from 70 percent in 1946/47 to 58 percent of its prewar level in 1947/48.[11] To prevent widespread starvation, the U.S. and, to a lesser extent, the U.K. financed huge imports of food. Nevertheless, the food rations actually issued frequently fell below the target of 1550 calories, in itself barely more than half the level of prewar consumption. In the first three years after the war, the development of external trade lagged even far behind the initially sluggish reconstruction of West Germany's internal economy. In 1947, West German imports amounted to 843 million dollars, with goods worth 600 million dollars being financed by foreign

---

[9] Investment 1947: 27 percent of its 1938 level, Krengel [1958], p. 98; industrial production: 34 percent, ECA [1951], p. 98.

[10] See Krengel [1958], pp. 16, 49–53.

[11] Statistisches Bundesamt [1953], p. 15.

aid, while exports stood at a meagre 318 million dollars.[12] This was all the more unfortunate since the disruption of almost all economic links between Western Germany and the Eastern half of the former Reich had reduced the opportunities for an internal division of labor. Hence, the need for economic exchanges with foreign countries was far greater than before the war.

On top of the Allied restrictions and the bureaucratic red tape, the monetary arrangements made sure that West German producers had little interest in exporting and that foreign customers · were rather reluctant to buy their goods. Apart from a minor foreign exchange retention quota introduced in Bizonia in September 1947, German firms were paid in almost useless Reichsmarks for their exports, while local markets offered at least opportunities for profitable barter transactions. Thus, firms had hardly any incentive to go beyond their export obligations.[13] Internally, a chaotic multiplicity of product-specific exchange rates was supposed to equate the fixed internal price of a good to the

---

[12] Bank deutscher Länder, Geschäftsbericht 1950, p. 46. The official numbers for overall exports may have to be adjusted upwards by up to 20 percent to account for widespread illegal trade at the borders. Interestingly, the typical pattern of smuggling was the import of money substitutes such as coffee and cigarettes for exports of high-quality and low-weight manufactures such as clocks, cameras and optical instrument; Motz [1954], p. 68. During the postwar misery, sound money was obviously needed more than anything else.

[13] The almost ridiculously painstaking administrative control did not help to make exporting look like an attractive option either. For example, a West German manufacturer of leather goods who had secured 17 export orders worth 2000 dollars at the Cologne fair in fall 1947 reportedly had to fill in 1343 forms, 561 of which were translations into English; Meyer [1953], pp. 258–285.

corresponding price on the world market (0.24–0.80 dollars per Reichsmark). Externally, West Germany was integrated from 1947 onwards into the network of bilateral trade treaties that governed almost the entire West European trade.

The change for the better was prepared by a political reassessment of the European economic and political situation, most of all in Washington. In 1947, the recovery of Western Europe as a whole was jeopardized by a major transatlantic balance-of-payments crisis. In the U.S., the exceptionally huge European balance-of-payments deficit was correctly interpreted as being in part caused by the virtual absence of the continent's traditional industrial heartland, Germany, from European trade circuits. Politically, the unresolved state of affairs and the economic distress in the center of Europe was seen as playing into the hands of local communist parties and the Soviet Union. With communists pushing their way into power in the East European countries occupied by the Soviet Union, the Western Allies finally decided to disregard Soviet reservations and go ahead with rebuilding the economy in their three zones of occupation and—if necessary—to establish a separate West German state. By 1948, with the abandonment of the original Allied policy, the time had come to put the economy in the three Western zones on a sound footing.

II. The Liberal Reforms of June 1948

1. The Reform Package

The move towards a sound economic system consisted of three separate reforms; namely, the currency reform and the so-called little tax reform, both of which had been basically worked out by the Western Allies for the three Western zones as a whole, and the reinstitution of a market economy in the U.S.-British "Bizone" in late June 1948.

The actual *currency reform* was enacted by the three Military Governments on June 20, 1948. [14] It comprised three major steps; namely, (i) a drastic contraction of the money supply by the introduction of the "Deutsche Mark" replacing the "Reichsmark," (ii) a restructuring and consolidation of existing private and public debt, and (iii) the establishment of strong institutional safeguards against future inflationary policies.

(i) A strictly limited amount of cash could be exchanged into D-Marks at a rate of 1:1. As an initial endowment, every individual thus received 40 DM immediately and a further 20 DM two months later. Firms were granted an allowance of 60 DM per employee, while public authorities received the equivalent of one month's revenue. All private cash balances and bank deposits, including savings accounts and time deposits, exceeding these allowances were to be scaled down by a factor of ten. [15] Half of this amount was immediately available, i.e., after the income tax office had checked the registered sums for prior tax evasion. The fate of the blocked half was decided in late September, with 35 percent (of the original total) being cancelled, 10 percent being released and 5 percent being credited to a special account for investment purposes. Thus, the

---

[14] For a detailed description of the prehistory of the currency reform and of the measures enacted, see Möller [1976], pp. 433–484, and Buchheim [1988], pp. 189–231.

[15] The respective deposits of public authorities were cancelled altogether.

effective conversion rate turned out to be 10: 0. 65 instead of 10: 1 for Reichsmark balances exceeding 600 RM. [16]

(ii) While the official prices and all recurrent payments like wages, rents and social security payments remained unchanged (1 RM = 1 DM), almost all debts were devalued by a factor of ten. The Reichsmark balances and the Reich bonds held by the commercial banks were wiped out. Instead, the banks received low-interest "equalization claims" amounting to roughly 4 percent of the Reich debt at the end of the war. [17] To restore their liquidity, the banks were granted deposits with the central banking system equal to 15 percent of their demand deposits plus 7. 5 percent of their time and savings deposits. As these reserves exceeded the new minimum requirements by 50 percent, the banks were thus given considerable leeway for credit expansion.

(iii) To protect the new currency, the Western Allies introduced two institutional safeguards against a future financing of public debt by money creation. First, with the currency reform, the Bank deutscher Länder became the sole provider of legal tender; contrary to the wishes of many German experts, the new central bank, which had been established in March 1948, was to be independent from the government and all other political bodies. [18] And second, the Military Government explicitly forbade excessive budget deficits. Art. 28 of the Conversion Law stated that "expenditures of public authorities must be covered by current income. The procurement of funds by means of

---

[16] For a detailed account, see Möller [1976].

[17] Gundlach [1987], p. 21.

[18] Möller [1976], p. 455; Müller [1982], p. 137.

credit shall be lawful only in anticipation of future revenues."[19]

A few days after the currency reform, the system of *central planning* was *abolished* in the Bizone. The guidelines on the decontrol of the economy ("Leitsätze") that the Bizonal parliament had passed on June 18, 1948, gave the head of the Bizonal economic administration, Ludwig Erhard, the right to liberalize most markets. Although the "Leitsätze" had not yet been approved by the Allied Bizonal Control Office,[20] Erhard lifted the price controls for almost all manufactured goods and some foodstuffs in the following week. And as Erhard did not renew the directives on the rationing of goods and the central allocation of resources that expired at the end of June,[21] the Bizonal economy started into the second half of 1948 with genuinely free markets in almost all goods for which the price controls had been removed. The most notable exceptions from the sweeping decontrol were basic foodstuffs, most raw materials (like coal, iron, steel and oil),[22] wages, rents and rates for basic public services like electricity, gas and water.

Simultaneously with the currency reform, the Military Governments enacted *changes in the tax system* geared towards promoting the formation of capital. Due to French objections, this tax reform was by no means as radical a

---

[19] Law No. 63, U.S. Zone, June 1948; WiGBl., 48. Beilage, No. 5, p. 19.

[20] The Bizonal Control Office did so on June 30, 1948.

[21] Buchheim [1988], p. 221.

[22] However, the administered prices for many of these goods were raised.

departure from the prohibitively high taxes on income—which the Allies had levied in 1946—as the German administration had demanded. With this "little tax reform,"[23] the top marginal income taxes which had stood as high as 95 percent in 1946[24] were cut by roughly one third, the corporate income tax was reduced from 65 to 50 percent and important tax exemptions were offered for income saved and invested. On the other hand, a high excise tax on coffee was introduced while many local taxes were substantially raised.[25]

Contrary to the drafts of German experts, the currency reform was not immediately complemented by a redistribution of wealth to achieve an equalization of war and postwar burdens ("Lastenausgleich").[26] Nevertheless, the "Lastenausgleich" may be counted as one of the 1948 reforms, as it was at least clear by mid-1948 that there would eventually be a such scheme.

---

[23] Mendershausen [1949], p. 659.

[24] Boss [1987], p. 4.

[25] Mendershausen [1949], p. 660.

[26] The first preliminary law on relief for the victims of the war, of expellation, the Nazi tyranny, and the currency reform was, however, not enacted prior to August 1949. The law on the "Lastenausgleich" proper was passed three years later. It provided for a special tax of 50 percent on all wealth holdings at the time of the currency reform, payable in yearly installments over the next decades. As the valuation clauses were very generous, much less than 50 percent of mid-1948 wealth was eventually redistributed; Schillinger [1985], pp. 283-290.

2. The Impact of the Reforms

The radical currency reform was an immediate and tremendous success. Virtually overnight, the Bizone took the great leap from the stage of primitive bilateral barter to that of genuinely multilateral exchange with money as the means of deferred payments. On the morning after the introduction of the Deutsche Mark, people accepted money in exchange for goods and labor services, the shop windows were full of products which had previously been unavailable—at least legally—and black and gray markets were reduced to an almost negligible role.

Soon after the reforms it became clear that the transformation of the country was not just due to shops putting goods on sale that they had previously hoarded or peddled illegally. In fact, production soared: In the second half of 1948, industrial output grew at an annualized rate of 137 percent, with the 1936-based index of production leaping from 50 in June to 57 in July and 77 in December.[27] Under the new regime, the incentive to work in factories rather than spending time in searching and bartering for food and other basic necessities was restored. While the industrial workforce grew by 13.1 percent, workers stayed

---

[27] Adjusted for number of working days; Ritschl [1985], p. 164. Abelshauser [1975] has cast doubt on the reliability of the official production indices, on which the positive assessment of the liberal reforms is based. Although the figures maybe somewhat distorted, Abelshauser's counterargument that they are heavily biased towards overstating the significance of the reforms of June 1948 has been convincingly refuted by Ritschl [1985] and Klump [1985].

on the job for 42.4 hours per week in December 1948, 4.2 hours longer than they had in June.[28]

Concurrent with the rise in the utilization of existing capacity, the postwar run-down of the physical capital stock was finally stopped. In the second half of 1948, the capital stock started to grow again at an annualized rate of 5.6 percent. Surprisingly, the investment surge could be funded, although private households—given the opportunity to convert cash balances and bank accounts into goods—had turned into net dissavers.[29] Aggregate investment was financed, above all, out of high business profits, but also out of foreign aid and the fiscal surplus of the public sector, which amounted to about 1.5 percent of GNP between the currency reform and the end of March 1949.[30]

Despite the spectacular advance of aggregate supply in real terms, the entire reform venture was actually put in jeopardy in fall 1948 by an unexpected surge in monetary demand. Prior to the currency reform, Erhard[31] and the Advisory Council to the Ministry of Economic Affairs[32] had predicted a deflation. However, both the money supply and the velocity of money increased by more than had been anticipated. The gradual conversion of old Reichsmark

---

[28] Wirtschaft und Statistik [1949/50], pp. 12–13, p. 157. In the following years, the work week lengthened even further to an average 46.5 hours in 1949 and 48.2 hours in 1950; Statistisches Bundesamt [1953], p. 506.

[29] Buchheim [1988], p. 229.

[30] Gundlach [1987], p. 29.

[31] See Müller [1982], p. 108.

[32] Wissenschaftlicher Beirat [1973], report of June 12, 1948, pp. 7–9, here: p. 7.

36

balances into D-Mark, the paying out of the second installment of the initial personal allowance and the considerable credit expansion in the banking system based on the generous initial endowments with central bank deposits made the quantity of money (M3) grow from 6.5 billion DM at the end of July to 10.4 billion DM three months later and 13.1 billion DM at the end of the year. [33] Furthermore, the velocity of money rose dramatically as firms managed to get along with surprisingly small cash balances while consumers looking at shop windows stocked with readily available goodies for the first time after more than five years saw little use for holding cash or saving money.

The unleashing of pent-up demand became almost instantaneously visible in prices. In the first four months after the reform, consumer prices (as measured by the cost of living index) grew at an annualized rate of 33.1 percent. Producer prices increased even more rapidly at an annual rate of 45 percent. [34] The fate of the new currency as well as the liberalization of markets was endangered. Both the inflation and the first administrative reaction, namely, to reduce the conversion rate for Reichsmark accounts into D-Marks from 10:1 to 10:0.65 on October 1, 1948, undermined public confidence in the new money. In fall 1948, first signs of an imminent repudiation of the paper

---

[33] Bank deutscher Länder, Monatsberichte, January 1949, p. 38; February 1949, p. 17, 38; own calculations.

[34] The difference was largely due to the fact that the former index includes housing rents, transport and other services for which the still administered prices remained constant, while the prices for most of those producers goods that remained under administrative control were raised.

money appeared, namely, a reemergence of bartering arrangements and a renewed hoarding of inventories. [35] On November 12, 1948, the trade unions called for a one-day general strike to protest against the inflationary consequences of Erhard's economic policies. Somewhat surprisingly, the major concern of the unions was inflation itself, not a genuine deterioration of the standard of living in real terms. Because of a roughly parallel increase in prices and nominal wages, the real purchasing power had not been diminished substantially in the postreform inflation. [36] Except for one token concession on which the Military Government insisted, namely, the establishment of a toothless independent price council, the West German authorities kept their nerves. In late 1948, the economy began to cool off. After the inflationary burst in summer and early fall, the price level was approaching the limit set by the monetary frame and the fiscal surplus. [37] Between October and December, the annualized increase of consumer prices dropped to 8.8 and that of producer prices to 2.9 percent. The final victory of the new currency became evident in the exchange rate against its commodity substitutes, i.e., in the prices of tobacco and coffee. On

---

[35] See Balabkins [1964], p. 115.

[36] Although wages remained under administrative control until early November, the Military government had authorized wage increases of 15 percent in late April 1948; Müller [1982], p. 152. This scope was almost completely exploited during the summer, so that wages did not lag far behind prices.

[37] In addition, the anticipation of the first Marshall Plan imports may have eased inflationary pressures; see Borchardt and Buchheim [1987], pp. 327 f.

December 15, 1948, these goods were traded for half of their prereform prices.[38]

When the postreform inflation abated in late 1948, a period of consolidation set in that lasted until early 1950. The growth of industrial production and GNP slowed down somewhat after the extraordinary surge in the second half of 1948 (annualized growth rates of industrial production: 137 percent in the second half of 1948, 24 percent in 1949 and roughly 12 percent in the first half of 1950). Remarkably, overall employment did not change dramatically in this period. While it had gone up by 230,000 jobs in the second half of 1948, some 150,000 jobs were lost in 1949. Hence, the spectacular advances in production could be attributed mostly to a rise in productivity per hour and in the number of working hours per week. As the labor force continued to increase rapidly due to the influx of refugees and expellees from the East, unemployment soared—despite the high real rates of growth—from 3.2 percent in June 1948 to a peak of 12.2 percent in March 1950.[39]

Nevertheless, the aggregate employment figures mask a massive reshuffling of labor between sectors. In the first six months after the reform, 370,000 jobs were lost in contracting sectors, while 600,000 jobs were created in expanding ones; in 1949, the employment gains of 260,000 jobs in the growing sectors were more than offset by losses of 410,000 jobs in shrinking ones. Never again would the speed of structural adjustment in the West German economy (as measured by changes in employment) be as high as in the early period.

---

[38] Wirtschaft und Statistik [1949/50], pp. 932 ff; own calculations.

[39] Paqué [1987], pp. 2 f.

In the second quarter of 1950, the period of consolidation gave way to a long phase of sustained employment growth, which brought the unemployment rate down to 3.4 percent by 1957. And the additional boost that the Korea boom imparted upon the West German economy in late 1950 and early 1951 finally put an end to the discussion whether an expansionary demand policy might be appropriate to reduce the high rates of unemployment. Thereafter, the stability-oriented macroeconomic policy of both the central bank and the federal government were not seriously questioned for quite some time.

In standard accounts of West Germany's economic history, the Marshall Plan (and the further Allied aid disbursements) are usually depicted as a major contribution to the miracle that started in the late 1940s. On the one hand, foreign aid significantly alleviated West Germany's balance-of-payments constraint until 1950. And given the dismal state of agriculture, the food deliveries were indeed a welcome supplement to domestic production. On the other hand, the aid receipts made it much easier for the West German (and Allied) authorities to stick to a gross overvaluation of West Germany's currency for the time being. [40] With less Allied red tape for exporters, a realistic valuation of the exchange rate and access to short-term credits on commercial terms to cushion the immediate J-curve effect of a thorough devaluation, West Germany would not have needed any aid to pay for her food imports. In any case, the Marshall Plan receipts cannot be counted as a major cause of the growth spurt that set in after the reforms of mid-1948. In fact, the first major shipments did not arrive until early 1949, i.e., at a time when the

---

[40] See Kostrzewa, Nunnenkamp and Schmieding [1989].

economy had already started to cool off again. And as far as the long-term importance of the Marshall Plan is concerned, one should note that major countries like the U.K. and France, which had received much more funds than West Germany, still fared far worse in the 1950s.

3. The Two Nonreforms

While the liberal reforms of June 1948 had been bold enough to initiate a period of extraordinarily rapid growth under the particular circumstances in West Germany at that time, it is important to note that major sectors of the economy were not decontrolled.

(i) Whereas the introduction of a unified exchange rate (0.3 dollars per D-Mark) in spring 1948 and the gradual abolition of the government monopoly over foreign trade were steps towards a more liberal trade regime, the external economy remained under tight state control well into the 1950s. When the Federal Republic was founded in late 1949, the conduct of cross-border transactions was in fact remarkably similar to the state of the internal economy before the reforms of June 1948: the repressed inflation and the subsequent lack of sound money had their counterparts in the overvaluation vis-à-vis the dollar and the ensuing shortage of international liquidity; the administrative control over prices and production and the internal barter trade was paralleled by the network of bilateral trade agreements between currency areas. The devaluation of European currencies against the dollar in late 1949 did not suffice to close the "dollar gap." Hence, Western Europe, including West Germany, took the long road towards currency convertibility and the abolition of bilateral quotas. Throughout the first half of the 1950s, most quantitative import restrictions were gradually lifted (in spite of the deliberalization during the balance-of-payments crisis which developed in the wake of the Korea boom). And by the end of 1958, the D-Mark became formally convertible for both current and capital account transactions. Although West Germany thus turned into a comparatively open country during the 1950s, the slow pace of progress in the external economy was in stark contrast to the more radical internal reforms of June 1948.[41]

(ii) Internally, the capital market—and the goods and service sectors listed above—were not liberalized thoroughly in the first years after the currency reform. Hence, firms had to rely on the self-financing of investment to a large extent.

III. The Lessons for Central and Eastern Europe

In many respects, before June 1948, West Germany resembled a textbook-example of a Soviet-type economy. Externally, foreign trade was a government monopoly; with regard to the internal economy, the system of central planning and the monetary overhang had resulted in an extremely inefficient allocation of resources and a widespread repudiation of the official currency. Note however that the central administration did not function well even according to its own standards. As the war-time discipline faded away in the years 1945–1948, West Germany

---

[41] Note that the rapid growth in West Germany's exports after 1948 does not imply that the external value of the currency was more or less correct. The growth rates look impressive mainly because exports had to start from an abysmally low level.

had turned into a kind of mixed economy in which central planning and decentralized decision-making overlapped. Hence, prior to the reforms of June 1948, West Germany may have had less in common with a Soviet-type economy proper than with what may emerge out of such a system after the first timid reform steps, most notably after a partial decentralization in the face of still grossly distorted relative prices.

Some general lessons from West Germany's experience are fairly obvious:

(1) While a mere softening of the rigid system of central administration may do more harm than good, a sudden and radical regime switch towards a market economy—including both a macroeconomic stabilization and a microeconomic liberalization—can initiate a sustained growth spurt.

(2) Even if output is growing considerably, a surge in inflation may jeopardize the success of the regime switch. Hence, it pays to keep the monetary reigns tight.

(3) Many of the sectors of the West German economy that were not liberalized in mid-1948 for supposedly social reasons were to cause serious political and economic problems later on, the most notable examples being agriculture, mining, transport and the housing market. Once the major parts of the economy had been decontrolled and once the nonliberalized sectors (and the general public) had become used to the special treatment for some sectors of the economy, it turned out to be very difficult to gather sufficient political support for a further liberalization. Hence, a reform package should encompass as many sectors as possible.

Yet, it is important to note six major differences between postwar West Germany and Central and Eastern Europe today:

(1) Despite the deterioration in the 1945–48 period, West Germany's sizeable capital stock incorporated up-to-date technology. Because of some war damages and—more importantly—the lunatic economic system, the economy was temporarily working well below its actual capacity, with factories churning out only roughly one third of what they had produced a few years ago. Once the incentive to invest was restored, comparatively few repair investments sufficed to put large parts of the capital stock and the modern infrastructure to use again. The countries of Central and Eastern Europe will need considerably more new capital to attain similar increases in production.

(2) Unlike the situation in Soviet-type economies, the means of production had remained—at least nominally—in private hands. Within the rigid frame set by the economic legislation of the time, the quest for private profitability and for keeping one's own firm intact could play a role in addition to the overriding imperative of meeting the prescribed targets. In sociological terms, this meant that entrepreneurs as a social group (or class) had not vanished. In Central and Eastern Europe, the dominance of state ownership of the means of production and the high degree of monopolization are likely to impair the responsiveness of the economies to market signals. Even if prices were liberalized and decision-making decentralized, these steps might not help all that much as long as managers are not controlled and rewarded by proprietors—or by economic agents who have an incentive to act as if they owned the firm.

(3) In West Germany, the institutional infrastructure of a market economy was still in place. In a broad sense, this institutional infrastructure encompasses, inter alia, a differentiated banking system, company laws and the accumulated experience that expresses itself in patterns of

behavior and in ways of conducting business and running firms, for instance, in accounting practices. In Germany, a system of central planning had merely been superimposed onto the highly developed market economy of the 1920s and early 1930s. Once the system of central planning was cleared away, the institutions of a market economy resurfaced.

(4) West Germany had been subject to fixed prices and a noticeable degree of central planning for a dozen years only, not for four or even six decades. Hence, economic agents were still familiar with the working of market forces. Furthermore, the structure of production had not yet adapted completely to the inherent underspecialization of centrally planned economies. Therefore, the structure of production will probably have to undergo much more sweeping changes in the countries of Central and Eastern Europe in order to correct the present distortions than in West Germany four decades ago. And even Germany's war-time bias towards armaments production had not created a major adjustment burden as the switch back to the traditional strength of the German economy, the production of (civilian) capital goods turned out to be fairly easy.

(5) The major structural distortion in postwar West Germany had been a skewed distribution of labor, not a grand-scale misallocation of capital. As most refugees and expellees had found temporary shelter in the countryside and as the dramatic shortage of food had made working and living there relatively attractive, the rural labor force had grown out of proportion immediately after the war. Furthermore, the allocation of manpower had been grossly distorted by restrictions on labor mobility, the conscription of workers for specific activities and, most importantly, the absurdities of a system in which money wages were almost meaningless. Nevertheless, West Germany had a rudimentary

labor market in which unemployment was not an uncommon feature. In Soviet-type economies, workers may have got used to the idea of an automatic "right to work." Work discipline and hence productivity in the ex-socialist countries may not increase sufficiently unless workers have to face the prospect of losing their job.

(6) External economic relations played a much smaller role for West Germany in the late 1940s than they do for Central and Eastern Europe today. West Germany's exports were negligible until the early 1950s. And because of the unresolved issue of the external indebtedness of the late Reich (which was finally settled by the London Debt Agreement of early 1953), the country had virtually no access at all to the rather tiny international capital market of that time.

The first five points imply that in 1948 West Germany could start from a much better basis than Central and Eastern Europe today. Sure enough, the ex-socialist countries will be able to reap the benefits of a transition from bilateral barter to multilateral exchange once they offer their citizens a trustworthy currency. Furthermore, the capital and labor productivity may increase considerably once necessary inputs can be bought on free markets any time they are needed. Unlike West Germany however, the countries of Central and Eastern Europe will have to lay the foundation of a capitalist economy by establishing the appropriate institutions and by privatizing state-owned firms before they can expect anything like an "economic miracle." Due to the lack of a capital market, resolving the question of how to accommodate dispossessed previous owners and, most importantly, due to the sheer size of the task, the privatization of state-owned firms is likely to be time-consuming. In the meantime, the ex-socialist countries should look for ways to make firms behave as if they were privately owned already. As a first step, it should be made clear who has the authority to take managerial decisions—including the dismissal of workers—after the de jure or at least de facto breakdown of the central economic administration. Next, the present—or the newly installed—managers should be given a noticeable incentive to maximize the future market value of their firms. For example, managers could be guaranteed a fixed share in the future privatization proceeds. The same could apply to the administrators of the state agency in charge of the actual privatization so that they have a personal interest in searching for the highest bidder.

Given the dismal state of the infrastructure and the limited resources of the public sector, the ex-socialist countries could invite domestic and foreign private firms to build and run major parts of the transport and telecommunications infrastructure as a normal business. Naturally, the firms would have to be allowed to charge their customers market rates. More precisely, the state could invite tenders for building and running specified parts of the infrastructure and choose the bidder who offers the best mix of high quality and low user fees.

The differences between West Germany in 1948 and Central and Eastern Europe today have further important implications:

(1) In 1948, West Germany had no choice but to eliminate the gigantic monetary overhang, either by open inflation or by a genuine currency reform, i.e., by devaluing existing money assets. Those ex-socialist countries which (still) suffer from the same malaise, most notably the USSR, have a third option at hand: they could use the proceeds of the privatization of state assets to soak up the surplus money before they liberalize prices. Unfortunately, this procedure has two major drawbacks: As the sale of firms (plus land

and apartments) will take time, the regime switch could be delayed considerably; and in the absence of genuine markets, the prices for the sale of state assets would have to be fixed rather arbitrarily. Yet, there is a convenient way out:[42] instead of devaluing money holdings, the state could convert cash balances exceeding certain limits into interest-bearing bonds that would be repaid after, say, five years out of the future privatization revenue; thus, highly liquid assets would be turned into less liquid ones.[43] This approach has the advantage that it can be implemented rapidly and easily without devaluing the savings of the population. Note, however, that the privatization proceeds can be spent only once: to the extent that they are used to avoid a genuine currency reform, they are no longer available for financing a budget deficit or for paying a "reform dividend" to the general public.

(2) With the need to rebuild major parts of the capital stock virtually from scratch, the countries of the latter region can hardly afford not to install a functioning capital market or—as West Germany did—to keep the fledgling capital market under tight control. The more structural change there has to be, the less feasible is the option of relying mostly on the self-financing of existing firms. Given the urgent need for capital inflows from abroad and for an efficient allocation of capital internally, the reformers

-----

[42] See Schmieding [1990].

[43] The velocity of money after the regime switch is hard to predict. In case the warranted quantity of money has been underestimated, i.e., in case too much cash has been converted into bonds, the money supply could quickly be adjusted by ordinary open market policy, i.e., by central bank purchases of some of the newly created bonds.

should not spend much time devising their own national banking systems and capital market regulations. Instead, they should state that EC rules will apply as of the end of 1992 at latest. In the meantime, these countries could import regulations (and regulators) from any thriving Western capital market and adjust the rules to local needs by implementing some courageous simplifications.

(3) More importantly, in 1948 West Germany could opt for separating the domestic deregulation from the external liberalization of the economy without damaging its growth prospects too much. Given the much greater dependence of Central and Eastern Europe on cross-border exchanges today and the need to keep domestic (state) monopolies in check by exposing them to competition from abroad, the regime switch has to encompass both the domestic and the external economy. Hence, currency convertibility, the dissolution of the state monopoly in foreign trade and the abolition of the most damaging restrictions on foreign trade (quotas, prohibitive tariffs) and payments should already go along with the internal deregulation. In the short run, this exposure to external competitors may be painful, as it is bound to speed up the process of structural change considerably; in the medium run, however, openness vis-à-vis the world may even be as beneficial for the ex-socialist countries as it was for West Germany at the time of its export boom in the 1950s. Given the proximity of the fully developed West European market, the scope for a rapid growth of Central and East European exports is considerable.

(4) As the mobility of capital and skilled labor has increased considerably over the last forty years, direct taxes will have to be reduced even more courageously in Central and Eastern Europe today than they were in West Germany in 1948. Otherwise, the ex-socialist countries

might not attract foreign capital in sufficient quantities and even face a brain drain.

All in all, the ex-socialist countries have three major disadvantages in comparison with West Germany at the time of the currency reform; namely, the dismal state of the capital stock, the lack of private enterprises and the need to establish the institutional framework of a market economy almost from scratch. Consequently, the regime switch from central planning to a market economy is not likely to cause an immediate growth spurt comparable to the early phase of West Germany's "Wirtschaftswunder." Instead, the adjustment is bound to be more painful and protracted. Nevertheless, the ex-socialist countries have one major opportunity that West Germany did not have: access to a well-functioning international capital market. Once the reforms have progressed far enough and once the economic and political uncertainties of the early period of the adjustment crisis are over, Central and Eastern Europe could successfully tap the savings of the world to build up a modern and highly productive capital stock within a few years.

Finally, there may be a political lesson to be learned from the experience of West Germany. It has sometimes been asserted that a turnaround in economic policy as tough and sweeping as the German liberal reforms of late June 1948 would have been next to unfeasible in a genuine democracy. However, the most contentious part of the reforms, namely, the sudden decontrol of most parts of the economy, had been endorsed by two German parliamentary bodies, the Economic Council (the representatives of the freely elected state parliaments of the Bizone) and the Länderrat (the representatives of the Bizonal state governments). Although a majority of West Germans did favor the reintroduction of price controls at the height of the postreform inflation, public opinion changed once the initial upheaval was over. In late 1948, the parties of the Bizonal "Frankfurt coalition," which had backed Erhard, increased their share of the popular vote in local elections in the British zone. More importantly, the theme of free markets versus a return to administrative control became the dominant issue in the campaign for the elections to the first West German Bundestag in mid-1949. Contrary to the expectations of many observers, the "Frankfurt coalition" gained the upper hand against the Social Democrats. With a liberal reform radical enough to attract widespread attention and to confer noticeable benefits on a great number of people, the conservative and liberal parties had paved their way to become the dominant combination of forces in West German politics for almost two decades. Hence, to be bold and to risk short-run unpopularity may ultimately pay off handsomely at the polls.

References

ABELSHAUSER, Werner, *Wirtschaft in Westdeutschland 1945-1948*. Stuttgart 1975.

BALABKINS, Nicolas, *Germany under Direct Controls*. New Brunswick, N.J., 1964.

BANK DEUTSCHER LÄNDER, *Geschäftsberichte*. Frankfurt am Main, various issues.

BANK DEUTSCHER LÄNDER, *Monatsberichte*. Frankfurt am Main, various issues.

BORCHARDT, Knut, and Christoph BUCHHEIM, "Die Wirkung der Marshallplan-Hilfe in Schlüsselbranchen der deutschen Wirtschaft." In: *Vierteljahreshefte für Zeitgeschichte*, Vol. 35, 1987, pp. 317-348.

BOSS, Alfred, Incentives und Wirtschaftswachstum—Zur Steuerpolitik in der frühen Nachkriegszeit, Institut für Weltwirtschaft, Kiel Working Paper No. 295, August 1987.

BUCHHEIM, Christoph, "Die Währungsreform 1948 in Westdeutschland." In: *Vierteljahreshefte für Zeitgeschichte*, Vol. 36, 1988, pp. 189-231.

ECONOMIC COOPERATION ADMINISTRATION (ECA), *Thirteenth Report to Congress of the Economic Cooperation Administration for the quarter ended June 30, 1951*. Washington 1951.

EHRET, Rolf G., *Der Weg zur Vollbeschäftigung in der Bundesrepublik Deutschland—Eine Studie über die Problematik der Vollbeschäftigung unter Berücksichtigung sowohl der theoretischen als auch der politisch-historischen Aspekte*. Winterthur 1959.

GUNDLACH, Erich, Währungsreform und wirtschaftliche Entwicklung: Westdeutschland 1948, Institut für Weltwirtschaft, Kiel Working Paper No. 286, April 1987.

KLUMP, Rainer, *Wirtschaftsgeschichte der Bundesrepublik Deutschland*. Wiesbaden 1985.

KOSTRZEWA, Wojciech, Peter NUNNENKAMP and Holger SCHMIEDING, A Marshall Plan for Middle and Eastern Europe? Institut für Weltwirtschaft, Kiel Working Paper No. 403, December 1989.

52

KRENGEL, Rolf, *Anlagevermögen, Produktion und Beschäftigung in der Industrie im Gebiet der Bundesrepublik 1924–1956*. Berlin 1958.

MENDERSHAUSEN, Horst, "Prices, Money and the Distribution of Goods in Postwar Germany." In: *American Economic Review*, Vol. 39, 1949, pp. 646–672.

MEYER, Fritz W., "Der Außenhandel der westlichen Besatzungszonen Deutschlands und der Bundesrepublik 1945–1952." In: Albert HUNOLD (ed.), *Wirtschaft ohne Wunder*. Zürich 1953, pp. 258–285.

MÖLLER, Hans, "Die westdeutsche Währungsreform von 1948." In: DEUTSCHE BUNDESBANK (ed.), *Währung und Wirtschaft in Deutschland 1876–1975*. Frankfurt am Main 1976, pp. 433–483.

MOTZ, Walter, *Die Regelung des Außenhandels in Deutschland 1945–1949*. Lörrach 1954.

MÜLLER, Georg, *Die Grundlegung der westdeutschen Wirtschaftsordnung im Frankfurter Wirtschaftsrat 1947–1949*. Frankfurt am Main 1982.

PAQUE, Karl-Heinz, Labour Surplus and Capital Shortage, German Unemployment in the First Decade after the Currency Reform, Institut für Weltwirtschaft, Kiel Working Paper No. 290, July 1987.

RITSCHL, Albrecht, "Die Währungsreform von 1948 und der Wiederaufstieg der westdeutschen Industrie." In: *Vierteljahreshefte für Zeitgeschichte*, Vol. 33, 1985, pp. 136–165.

RÖPKE, Wilhelm, "Offene und zurückgestaute Inflation: Bemerkungen zu Jacques Rueffs L'Ordre Social." In: *Kyklos*, Vol. 1, 1947, pp. 57–71.

———, "Das Deutsche Wirtschaftsexperiment: Beispiel und Lehre." In: SCHWEIZER INSTITUT FÜR AUSLANDS-FORSCHUNG (ed.), *Vollbeschäftigung, Inflation und Planwirtschaft*. Zürich 1951, pp. 261–312.

SCHILLINGER, Reinhold, *Der Entscheidungsprozeß beim Lastenausgleich 1945–1952*. St. Katharinen 1985.

SCHMIEDING, Holger, "Geldreform im Spätsozialismus: Eine fast schmerzlose Währungsreform—Wie die DDR sogar Ludwig Erhard übertreffen könnte." In: *Neue Zürcher Zeitung*, January 17, 1990, p. 18.

STATISTISCHES BUNDESAMT, *Statistisches Jahrbuch*. Wiesbaden, various issues.

STATISTISCHES AMT DES VEREINIGTEN WIRTSCHAFTS-GEBIETES, *Wirtschaft und Statistik*. Wiesbaden, various issues.

WALLICH, Henry C., *Mainsprings of the German Economic Revival*. New Haven 1955.

WINIECKI, Jan, *The Distorted World of Soviet-Type Economies*. London 1988.

WISSENSCHAFTLICHER BEIRAT BEIM BUNDESMINISTERIUM FÜR WIRTSCHAFT, *Sammelband der Gutachten von 1948 bis 1972*. Göttingen 1973.

Jan Winiecki

How It All Began: Sources of the Recent Breakdown
of the Soviet Economic System

I. Introduction

The "Spring of Nations" that took much of East-Central
Europe by storm last autumn was without doubt a political
phenomenon. An apparent abandonment of the doctrine of
military intervention in subordinated East-Central Europe by
the Gorbachev regime had encouraged change for some time.
The Hungarian decision to dismantle border fortifications at
the border with Austria triggered a flood of East German
refugees to the West that put pressure on the East German
communist regime. Once Honecker fell, Czechoslovak
neo-stalinists found themselves isolated and the pressure
applied skillfully by the opposition resulted in the smoothest
possible transfer of power. The fall of Ceausescu completed
the domino effect.

But all these spectacular phenomena, coupled with the
unfolding of *glasnost* and *perestroika* in the Soviet Union
itself have been outcomes of long processes rather than
spasmodic events as they often seemed to outsiders. And,
the processes were mainly economic in nature. This author
warned years ago that Soviet-type economies were entering
an era of long-term decline. [1]

There have been other determinants of change:
ecological, social, demographic, etc. They all combined into
what this author called quite recently "the irreversible

---

[1] See Winiecki [1984].

multifaceted decline of the Soviet system. "[2] It is this irreversible decline and responses to it by societies living under the system that have been instrumental in bringing about changes in East-Central Europe and the Soviet Union itself. Let us follow the varied economic phenomena that all contributed, simultaneously or successively, to the downfall of that wasteful monstrosity.

II. Sources of Economic Decline Endogenous to the Soviet Economic System

What is worth stressing at the start is the endogeneity of the sources of economic decline. When the first signs of increased disturbances and decline appeared in the 1970s some analysts, especially those sympathetic to the system, were pointing at the disturbances in the world economy as the source of the problems encountered by Soviet-type economies. They were never able to explain, however, why signs of stress and decline were as strong (if not stronger) in the Soviet Union, the net winner of two so-called oil crises, than in the smaller East-Central European countries.

More perceptive was the view that the disturbances in the world economy exacerbated the distortionary, if not self-destructive, features of the Soviet-type economies.[3] To begin with, the traditionally stressed distorted motivation in Soviet-type economies that results, inter alia, in abnormally high levels of resource use became increasingly painful since the first oil price jump and commodity boom of the early 1970s.

---

[2] See Winiecki [1989].

[3] See Winiecki [1984] and [1987a], p. 16.

Quite obviously, with consumption of energy or steel per one dollar of GDP being 2–2.5 times higher in Soviet-type economies than in market-type economies, the former began to feel the cost of their high resource intensity much more strongly than before. Moreover, while saddled with a high resource intensity, Soviet-type economies, except the Soviet Union, have been facing a relative fall in domestic resource availability. It meant that these countries had to import more and more of their energy and industrial mineral inputs.

Although smaller Soviet-type economies obtained a large part of their imported inputs from the USSR, costs of obtaining these resources in the latter also rose sharply. Consequently, rulers of Soviet-type economies faced a dilemma. With resource imports from the USSR leveling off and later declining and imports from the world market difficult to pay for, due to weak export performance, their economies had a choice of either declining or undergoing a far-reaching change that would reduce resource intensity. This dilemma is shown graphically in Figure 1.

Summing up, an old weakness of the Soviet economic system became a matter of much greater urgency. High resource intensity emerged in the 1970s as a strong growth-inhibiting factor.

Much less known, let alone estimated quantitatively, is what this author called the twofold underspecialization of Soviet-type economies. [4] It is the result of the Soviet style industrialization strategy and features specific to the Soviet economic system. The gist of the "steep ascent" strategy was maximization of investment in the industrial sector in order to achieve the largest possible increase in its share

---

[4] See Winiecki [1987b].

Figure 1: The Actual Pattern of Change of Energy Intensity
in Market-Type Economies (M) and Alternative
Future Paths of Energy Intensity in Soviet-Type
(and post-Soviet-type) Economies

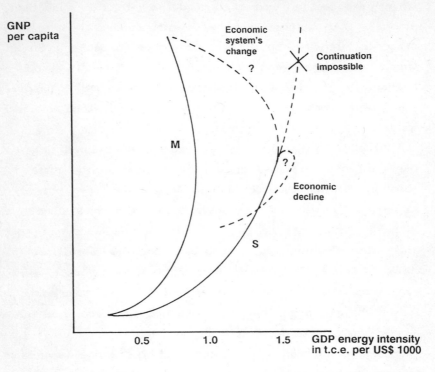

of output in the shortest possible time span (all this
conducted under near autarchic conditions). Investment
within the industrial sector was in turn concentrated on
heavy industry because it was assumed that without the
capability to produce machinery and equipment, Soviet-type
economies would not be able to overcome their backwardness
(that they would become backward machinery producers was
not the possibility envisaged at the time!).

This strategy, devised for the Soviet Union and later
implanted in the smaller Soviet-type economies, was
nonsensical from the start in the case of the latter. The
foregone benefits of international specialization for small

countries trying to produce as much as possible domestically resulted in an oversized industrial sector. This sector, however, has been decreasingly able to satisfy internal demand, since each new final good requires a range of new intermediate products for its manufacture at high cost due to the smallness of the internal market. The issue of an import-substitution-based development strategy has been well researched with respect to developing countries.[5] So it will only be noted that the degree of separation from the world market has been greater in Soviet-type economies than in LDCs, with correspondingly larger structural distortions.

But even more important were system-specific features of underspecialization. With central planning breeding excess demand, uncertainty and shortage, enterprises have been adjusting their behavior accordingly, trying to produce as much as possible of the intermediate inputs they need within the enterprise. In other words, enterprises in Soviet-type economies also pursue an "import" substitution strategy, substituting their own high cost production for unreliable supplies ("imports") from other domestic enterprises.

However irrational in macroeconomic terms, such behavior makes sense for enterprises that need these inputs to fulfill their plan targets with respect to final output in order to obtain premiums and bonuses. For they are reasonably sure that cost overruns will be compensated one way or another by superior bodies in the bureaucratic hierarchy.

The effects of this microlevel "import" substitution running counter to the fundamental economic logic and the

---

[5] See the strand of literature starting with Little et al. [1970] and Balassa et al. [1971].

established pattern of industrial specialization were especially severe. Since Adam Smith it has been recognized that growing wealth is achieved through increased specialization. Under central planning, however, real gains from the expanded division of labor—as more and more separable processes are carried out by firms specializing in them—have slowed down or were even reversed. The result was a hypertrophy of the industrial sector that in Soviet-type economies grew to much above the share in total output and employment typical for market-type economies at any level of economic development (see Figure 2).

Figure 2: Changes in the Shares of Industry in GDP and Employment in Market-type Economies (M) and Soviet-type Economies (S) in Accordance with the Changes in GNP per Capita

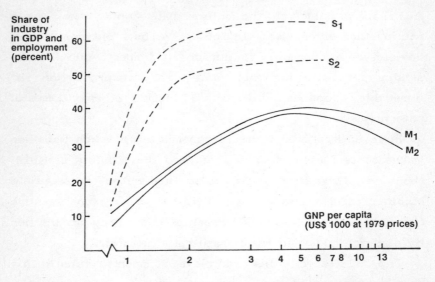

This was one of the important reasons of the *growth-without-much-prosperity* phenomenon visible in Soviet-type economies almost from their beginnings. It again became costlier as Soviet-type economies shifted their attention to

more sophisticated, technologically advanced goods in the 1970s.

However, before this author turns to the intertwined problems of underspecialization, inflexibility of Soviet-type hierarchical bureaucracies and slowness to innovate, two important aspects of underspecialization should be stressed here.

First, Soviet-type economies not only forego (a large) part of the gains from the first industrial revolution, i.e., inter-enterprise specialization in production of goods within the quickly expanding market, but also the gains from the present industrial revolution. An important component of the latter is a rapidly growing specialization in the production of business services previously performed mostly within the industrial enterprises.

Also, the long neglect of a service sector, traditional and modern alike, has begun to affect more strongly the performance of Soviet-type economies. Undersized and long starved of resources, the service sector turned into an ever-stronger drag on economic growth. Especially since the mid-1970s, when ruling groups devoted more and more resources to propping up the declining performance of industry, the infrastructure of these economies began to decay at an accelerated rate. Low quality inputs require extensive replacement and maintenance activities also in the service sector. Without quantitatively large supplies, the reliability of services fell dramatically. To give but one example, the breakdown rate of main water pipes in the USSR in 1976–1980 period was equal to 40 accidents per 100 km annually. This absurdly high rate increased to 100 accidents per 100 km annually in the next five-year period![6]

_____

[6] Ekonomicheskaya Gazeta [1988].

The disadvantages of the hierarchical economic bureaucracy in the Soviet economic system have been long recognized as a disadvantage. But again, it is the turn of the 1960s and 1970s that changed the old weakness into a fatal flaw. In this author's opinion, the shift in the role of the engine of economic growth from economy-of-scale-based to flexible, entrepreneurial and innovation-based industries has been at the source of the marked change for the worse.[7]

If there ever existed an advantage of the Soviet-type economy over the market-type economy, it would be the former's capability to quickly (and often ruthlessly) collect resources and allocate them for the implementation of a few large projects. This capability gave Soviet-type economies an appearance of efficiency, as they were able to build large-scale plants: steel mills, cement plants, fertilizer plants, etc. The speed of allocation and collection in spite of the attendant waste allowed Soviet-type economies to catch up in some respects with Western market-type economies.

All this changed with the shift of the growth engine role to industries based on flexibility and other features antithetical to central planning. When Soviet-type economies began to expand less material-using, more value-added industries, so that a multitude of new products and more sophisticated versions of the old ones began to be manufactured, the sharply raised requirements of smooth management of complex coordination processes became too great a burden for the slow-moving bureaucracy. Signs of strain multiplied.

---

[7] See Winiecki [1987a], pp. 18–19.

It is worth noting that technology imports, which were supposed to circumvent the barrier of hierarchical bureaucratic management, itself adverse to innovation, did not help much. On the contrary, the new and higher quality standards of products manufactured under Western licenses put an additional burden on domestic suppliers of inputs to these products. They required additional imports, upsetting foreign trade balances, and causing quickly increasing indebtedness. The only exception was the Soviet Union enjoying windfall gains from two very large oil price increases (but even that country could have used its gains in a different way, were it not for the extra import demand for Western intermediate inputs). It turned out that bad innovators are also bad imitators.[8] Soviet-type economies found themselves under yet another pressure: increasing demand for imports in the face of the weak ability to export.

This ability to export to the world market, particularly to export manufactures, has been not only weak but declining over time. The case of Czechoslovakia is the most telling one. At the turn of century, the Czech lands of the Austro-Hungarian empire were one of the strongest world centers of heavy industry (steel making, engineering). In 1948, Czechoslovak engineering goods still fetched the same unit price as West German goods. By the mid-1960s, they were already receiving only half of the average unit price obtained by others on the EEC market. By the mid-1980s, they were receiving a dismal one-fourth. Other Soviet-type economies experienced similar declines as shown in Table 1. In other product groups, the situation was not as bad as in highly sophisticated engineering, but

---

[8] See Holzman [1979].

on the average more and more goods had to be exported to earn one unit of convertible currencies. These developments contributed significantly to the fall in real wages, quite apart from the consequences of indebtedness that emerged as another constraint.

Table 1: Unit (Kilogram) Prices of Engineering Goods Obtained by East European Members of COMECON on the EEC Market Relative to Average Prices Obtained by Exporters There in 1965–1985 (in percentage: average price equals 100 percent)

	1965	1970	1975	1977	1980	1985
COMECON (weighed average)	50	45	37	38	35	28
Bulgaria	32	39	36	34	30	25
Czechoslovakia	47	45	38	36	32	25
GDR*	58	47	48	44	37	33
Hungary	77	72	52	53	47	35
Poland	36	36	36	44	34	23
Rumania	37	39	38	45	38	29
USSR	46	43	30	30	29	23
*without the intra-German trade						

Source: E. D. Winiecki and J. Winiecki [1988].

III. Aggregate Effects of Decline: Much Worse Than Shown by Official Statistics

If official statistics in Soviet-type economies are taken seriously, then the adverse effects of the range of interrelated economic determinants of change should be regarded as surprisingly small. There was a slowdown in economic growth rates of Soviet-type economies since the late 1970s, but credulous analysts could still write, for example, that the growth record of Soviet-type economies used to be outstanding but now is merely good.[9] Those who knew better stressed for years, if not decades, that official figures grossly overestimated the real growth, sometimes by more than 50 percent.

American (C. I. A.) estimates, for example, pointed out that Soviet economic growth was nearer to two thirds of the officially published rates in the postwar (1950–80) period. U. N. estimates pointed to similar overstatements. It is due to *perestroika* that these downward revisions of official figures were revised downward even further by Soviet economists themselves. According to Khanin, Soviet economic growth was barely above 50 percent of the official figures in the 1961–1975 period, whereas in the next decade the economy stagnated (growth of less than 1 percent annually), while official figures showed a relatively good growth performance of 3. 5–4 percent annually.

A comparison of Soviet official, C. I. A. unofficial, and Russian economists' unofficial estimates is given in Table 2. Interestingly, Russian estimates are so unfavorable that bureaucrats from the Soviet statistical office defended themselves against lower Russian estimates, contrasting them with relatively better C. I. A. figures (which in the pre-*glasnost* era were dubbed anti-Soviet propaganda!).

A smaller effort was made to estimate the economic growth of Soviet East-Central European dependencies. But those that were made showed a range of figures lower than the officially published statistics, at times more than 50 percent lower.[10] The worst offenders in terms of the biggest discrepancies were East Germany, Rumania and

---

[9] See Weitzman [1987], p. vii.

[10] See ECE [1980] for the 1950–1973 period and T. P. Alton in Congress of the U. S. [1985] for the 1975–1982 period.

Table 2: Official Statistics and Varying Unofficial Estimates
of Annual Economic Growth Rates in the USSR,
1951–1985

Period	Official (1)	ECE (2)	CIA (3)	Unofficial Russian (4)
1951–55	-	5.1	7.6	-
1956–60	-	5.2	7.1	-
1951–60	10.2	-	-	7.2
1961–65	6.5	5.4	5.1	4.4
1966–70	7.7	4.4	5.6	4.1
1971–75	5.7	3.9[a]	3.7[b]	3.2
1976–80	4.2	-	2.6[b]	1.0
1981–85	3.5	-	-	0.6

[a] 1971–1973 only.
[b] Alternative CIA estimates are 2.3 % in 1976–80 and 1.9 %
in 1981–85, on annual basis (5).

Sources: (1) Soviet official statistics; (2) ECE [1980]; (3)
Congress of the U.S. [1982]; (4) Khanin [1988];
and (5) Congress of the U.S. [1987], pp. 126 ff.

Bulgaria. These countries stagnated at best, if not went
into decline. In fact, Polish statistics in the post-Solidarity
period also raised a lot of doubt. Instead of impressive 4–5
percent annual growth rate some estimates put it at 1–2
percent range at best.

If economic growth was lower than officially registered,
especially toward the end of the period, inflation was
higher—often much higher than published by the respective
statistical authorities. This stemmed from the well-known
phenomenon of hidden inflation in Soviet-type economies.
Various estimates pointed to a substantial—and rising—
hidden inflation. Accordingly, since hidden inflation
estimates were markedly higher than official figures of real
wage growth rates, Western studies confirmed Soviet-type
economy consumers' perception of declining real wages and

consumption. Both began to fall in the mid-1970s.[11] The decline was the steepest, of course, in Rumania and Poland but wages and consumption declined in every country.

Stagnating economies and falling real wages were coupled with increasing domestic imbalances. Except for Rumania, communist rulers were afraid of the social consequences of reverting to Stalinist confiscatory measures with respect to excess liquidity in the hands of the population. Consequently, forced savings began to grow faster than in the past.

Repressed inflation (shortages) became more visible as a result. Thus, not only private consumption fell, often quite strongly, as in Poland or Rumania, but also living standards declined due to longer queues. These developments, once they turned out to be a permanent feature of Soviet-type economies, became a determinant of decline in their own right. Noneconomic factors began to contribute to the accelerated decay of the Soviet economic system.

IV. Noneconomic Determinants of Decay

For societies living under the Soviet economic system, the most important direct effect was the fall in living standards. This entailed the fall in real wages and consumption (see the preceding section and Table 3), as well as the still less easily estimated fall in living conditions (deterioration of housing, municipal infrastructure,

---

[11] See Askanas [1985] for five Soviet-type economies. For least reliable Rumania and Bulgaria, it is indirect assessments that strongly confirm the same pattern.

Table 3: Monthly Average Real Wages in 5 Soviet-type Economies in 1965–1982 in 1975–Prices (1975=100)

Country	1965	1975	1980	1982
Czechoslovakia	92.6	100	98.6	96.1
GDR	103.2	100	95.0	90.9
Hungary	90.4	100	98.6	96.1
Poland	88.0	100	91.0	67.3
USSR	82.7	100	99.8	95.7

Source: Askanas [1985]

transportation and telecommunications, and—last but not least—of environmental conditions).

The continuing fall in living standards may well have convinced people living under communist rule that even the modest increases they had enjoyed since around the mid-1950s were over. Having formed such expectations, societies at large, not only individuals, have assumed that the system is hopelessly inefficient. As Wiles rightly stressed, years of broken promises brought about a widespread feeling in the Eastern part of Europe that "not just the economy but the whole theoretic system is not good."[12] The earliest sign of the extent of such feelings were heated public debates on the "reformability" of the Soviet economic system in Poland in 1980–1981.

Such expectations transformed into attitudes and hence into deteriorating work effort, once they set in, and became a separate, even if derived, determinant of decline affecting independently economic performance. Hopelessness begets cynicism and cynicism begets corruption, contributing to further deterioration.

---

[12] See Wiles [1982], p. 11.

There were some differences between Soviet-type economies in this respect. The dividing line was industrial tradition. In those Soviet-type economies that industrialized before communist rule, workers and bureaucrats simply would not perform below a certain (modest) level because they would not think it possible. On the other hand, in recently transformed, mainly peasant, societies, already low levels of performance would fall sharply to a much greater extent. Therefrom stem the differences in the extent of deterioration in work attitudes between Czechoslovakia, East Germany and, in part, Hungary, where these processes were less dramatic, and the remaining Soviet-type economies.

But sociopsychological consequences of falling living standards were only one aspect of the irreversible multifaceted decline that set in all over East-Central Europe and the USSR. Fast decline of urban infrastructure that made life in the cities decreasingly bearable has been affecting urban population in these countries in much the same way as the fall in consumption.

Less easily perceived but no less damaging in the long run was environmental pollution. It turned out that the centralized system is even less able to take remedial action in the cases of diverging social and individual returns. Unsubstantiated praises for authoritarian solutions to the contrary, [13] pollution in Soviet-type economies has been very much worse than elsewhere in the world. For example, East-Central Europe, excluding the Soviet Union, emitted in 1982 some 40.7 million tons of sulphur dioxide as compared

---

[13] See, for example, the nonsensical utterances of Kimball [1973], an American conservationist, about the ease with which the USSR protects its environment.

to 18.6 million tons for the EEC countries. The above figures are more poignant if one takes into account that the former countries have slightly smaller territory and one fourth to one half of the living standards of the latter. On a per capita basis, emissions in East Germany have been more than four times larger than those in West Germany, and so were those in Czechoslovakia relative to those in Austria.

Other sources of pollution, as well as damage caused by mining, hydroelectric dams and other projects, contributed also to a much greater extent than in other countries. The worst situation with respect to land, water and forest damages is probably in the Soviet Union. To give but one example, between one-fourth and one-half of the black soil in the Soviet Union has been destroyed since collectivization. [14] But again, elsewhere in Soviet-type economies, things were not much better. A recent report of Czech economists points out that 54 percent of agricultural land is threatened by erosion, while 80 percent by souring. [15]

It is not surprising under the circumstances that life expectancy has been on the decrease in the Eastern part of Europe for years if not decades. Again, the worst case is the Soviet Union itself. A Soviet male was expected at birth to live less than 60 years according to unpublished 1979 census data leaked to the West in the early 1980s. [16] Adult males live shorter and shorter in other Soviet-type

---

[14] See Antonow [1987].

[15] Source: Institute of Economics, Czechoslovak Academy of Sciences [1989].

[16] See Feshbach [1985].

economies as well. Hungary, Czechoslovakia and Poland registered the largest increases in mortality since the 1960s. The trend again accelerated in the 1980s. Figure 3 compares life expectancy in these countries with some Western countries. The dramatically diverging patterns of both groups of countries are there for all to see. Let me add that in other male age groups the situation is not any better. [17]

The combination of economic and noneconomic decline made the societies not only more vulnerable, as shown by falling life expectancy, but also ever more ready to criticize and challenge the ruling elites. This in turn put more stress on the ruling stratum in the Soviet system, for a sullen and rebellious population requires both more extensive and intensive control as tired Polish apparatchiks, security policemen and nomenklatura bureaucrats learned in the 1980s.

Thus, the costs of governance began to increase in the communist-ruled Eastern part of Europe. At the same time benefits from parasiting upon the Soviet economic system have declined. The ruling stratum has been able to continue to appropriate the rent from ruling through allocation of goods in short supply for themselves but even this has become more difficult. For example, in Poland cars allocated to the ruling stratum at below market prices were distributed less often in the 1980s than a decade earlier. And this took place in spite of the fact that Polish rulers almost doubled the share of cars distributed in that way from some 20 percent in the 1970s to almost 40 percent in the 1980s. The reason for the decline: falling production coupled with increased imports.

---

[17] The data are from Mantorska [1990].

Figure 3: Average Male Life Expectancy at the Age of 30 in
Selected Soviet-type and Market-type Economies

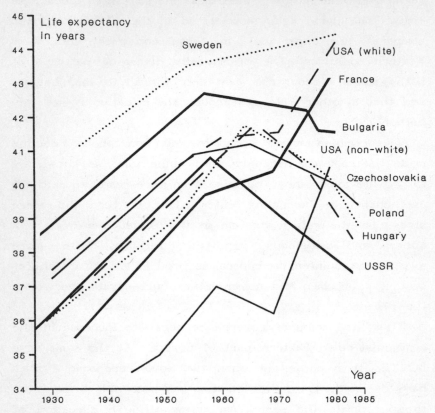

But the allocation of goods for the parasitic ruling
stratum was the least affected part of the good life of the
communist "privilegentsia" (to use the brilliant term coined
by the Economist). The degradation of the urban
infrastructure affected them much more strongly. Since
heating systems are centralized in the East, both old-age
pensioners and arrogant nomenklatura representatives have
shivered from cold and/or had to forego shaving for weeks
in row. It turned out to be much easier to allocate
cottages, cars, color TV-sets, etc., to themselves than to
avoid breakdowns of water, heating and sewage systems.

The best known case, which amounted to no less than the poetic justice, was the gaspipe breakdown that ruined of all places a part of the planning commission's building in Prague.

The consequences of the extraordinarily high levels of pollution could not have been avoided by the ruling stratum, either. A party secretary in a highly polluted Russian, Polish, Czech, or East German city has to breath the same air—containing a lot of sulphur, nitrogen, lead, cadmium (you name it)—as everybody else.

The consequences of systematic decay became increasingly a part of everyday life, not only for the ruled but also for the rulers. The Brezhnevs, Ceausescus, and Honeckers of the world did not notice it, of course. But policemen, lower echelon apparatchiks and bureaucrats and military officers—in other words the pillars of the system—might have repeatedly asked themselves whether they still benefited from their relative position under the conditions of steep absolute decline.

Moreover, as this author has stressed elsewhere, [18] not all segments of the ruling communist stratum have been equally strongly interested in maintaining the Soviet economic system. The police, but especially the military, have not been benefiting to the same extent from the system as did apparatchiks and bureaucrats. And when it became clearly visible that the system is not delivering what the military expects, i. e., modern weaponry in sufficient quantity and quality, members of the military were prepared to discard it more than others (if anywhere within the ruling stratum, it is among the professional military that Gorbachevites enjoy the strongest support). Soviet satellites

---

[18] See Winiecki [1987a] and more systematically [1990].

did not have imperial ambitions but their professional militaries also became more sensitive to the need for change. The performance of the Rumanian military is particularly telling in this respect.

V. The Inevitable Breakdown

As a result, not only the costs of governance have been on the increase for quite some time in Soviet-type economies but also the benefits from running the economy and the country were on the decline. Such a situation made the radical change increasingly probable. As this author wrote in the spring of 1989, "at a certain point understood graphically as an intersection of falling benefits from parasiting upon the inefficient economic system and raising costs of containing the increasingly hostile society, the ruling stratum will become ready to accept the "critical mass" of changes—including necessary political changes. "[19]

Once popular pressures grew, the whole edifice began to crack. The MANES, THEKELS, FARES, already visible for quite some time on the wall for those able and willing to see, suddenly caught the attention of leading writers, scholars and politicians everywhere in the Western world. But this new awareness was simultaneous with the breakdown itself.

---

[19] See Winiecki [1989].

References

ANTONOW, M., article in *Nauka i Technika*, translated into Polish in *Przeglad Techniczny*, No. 45, 1987.

ASKANAS, Benedykt, *Niveau und Entwicklung der Reallöhne in den RGW-Ländern im Vergleich mit Österreich*. Wiener Forschungsberichte, No. 103, 1985.

BALASSA, Bela A. and associates, *The Structure of Protection in Developing Countries*. Baltimore 1971.

CONGRESS OF THE U.S. (ed.), *USSR: Measures of Economic Growth and Development, 1950-80*. Studies prepared for the use of the Joint Economic Committee, Washington, D.C., 1982.

——, *East European Economies: Slow Growth in the 1980s*. Papers submitted to the Joint Economic Committee, Vol. 1, Washington, D.C., 1985.

——, *Gorbachev's Economic Plans*. Study Papers submitted to the Joint Economic Committee, Vol. 1, Washington, D.C., 1987.

EKONOMICHESKAYA GAZETA, No. 14, 1988.

FESHBACH, Murray, "The Age Structure of the Soviet Population: Preliminary Analysis of Unpublished Data." In: *Soviet Economy*, Vol. 1, 1985, pp. 177-193.

HOLZMAN, Franklyn D., "Some Systematic Factors Contributing to the Convertible Currency Shortages of Centrally Planned Economies." In: *American Economic Review*, Vol. 69, No. 2, 1979, pp. 76-80.

INSTITUTE OF ECONOMICS, CZECHOSLOVAK ACADEMY OF SCIENCES, Czechoslovakia on the Crossroad. A Report by a Collective of Authors, November 1989, mimeo (in Czech).

KHANIN, G., "Economic Growth: An Alternative Estimate." In: *Kommunist*, No. 17, 1988, pp. 83-90 (in Russian).

KIMBALL, T., "I Felt the Winds of Change." In: *National Wildlife*. February-March 1973.

MANTORSKA, T., *Demographic Situation in Areas under Ecological Threat*. Institute of Economics of the Polish Academy of Sciences, Research Monograph, 1990 (in Polish).

LITTLE, Ian M. D. , Tibor SCITOVSKY and Maurice SCOTT, *Industry and Trade in Some Developing Countries*. London 1970.

U. N. ECONOMIC COMMISSION FOR EUROPE (ECE), *Economic Bulletin for Europe*, Vol. 31, No. 2, 1980.

WEITZMAN, Martin L. , "Foreword." In: Padma DESAI, *The Soviet Economy: Problems and Prospects*. Oxford 1987, pp. vii-viii.

WILES, Peter, "Introduction: Zero Growth and the International Nature of the Polish Disease." In: Jan DREWNOWSKI (ed.), *Crisis in the East European Economy*. London 1982, pp. 7–17.

WINIECKI, Elisabeth D. , Jan WINIECKI, Intra-Branch Structural Change in Poland and Other COMECON Countries and Specialisation for the World Market, Main School for Planning and Statistics, Warsaw, November 1988, manuscript (in Polish).

WINIECKI, Jan, *Soviet-type Economies: Entering an Era of Long-Term Decline*. Warsaw 1984.

—— [1987a], *Economic Prospects: East and West*, Centre for Research into Communist Economies, London 1987.

—— [1987b], "The Overgrown Industrial Sector in Soviet-Type Economies: Explanations, Evidence, Consequences." In: *Comparative Economic Studies*, Vol. 28, No. 4, 1987, pp. 13-36.

——, "Der Preis der Privilegien und der Machterhaltung: Verfall auf der ganzen Linie ist der bestimmende Faktor für Wandel im Sowjetsystem." In: *Frankfurter Allgemeine Zeitung*, April 28, 1989.

——, "Why Economic Reforms Fail in the Soviet System: A Property Rights Approach." In: *Economic Inquiry*, Vol. 28, No. 2, 1990, pp. 195-221.

Václav Klaus

Main Obstacles to Rapid Economic Transformation of Eastern Europe: The Czechoslovak View

In the past decades, the citizens of East European countries (including Czechoslovakia) have experienced a gradual, but substantial loss of illusions concerning the potentials of a centrally planned economy (and society); the discontent of more than forty years of a planned, instead of an open, society (in the same sense as Popper) became visible in the dramatic year of 1989. The newly formed governments (with a popular mandate) now have the unique opportunity to transform their economies into normally functioning market economies of the Western type.

There are many obstacles to achieving this goal in the near future. One of the most significant is the lack of understanding of basic economic principles, of fundamentals that constitute a "given" in the Western world. Nonetheless, I would like to turn attention to more general questions, to the psychological (or attitudinal or ideological) aspects of the whole problem in the first part of the paper, and to outline the reform strategy of the new Czechoslovak government in the final part. Digression on the unreformed economic system is in the second part.

I. Ideological Puzzle

Overwhelming criticism of the existing economic and social system in a country like Czechoslovakia does not stem from the tradition of classical liberal thinking (in its true sense). This is dangerous because the debate about the future is marked by confusion based on various intellectual and ideological prejudices, on faulty and misplaced education, and on an insufficient departure from the tenets of the old collectivistic doctrine. I am afraid that a large part of the radical criticism is still connected with "rationalistic constructivism" (to use the Hayekian term), which is often implicitly considered to be an answer to many problems of the existing system. The recent comeback of several leading (and therefore ambitious) reformers of the 1960s from internal and external exile amplifies the relevance of this point.

What are the main platforms of the ideological approaches that influence the thinking of the reformers in the transitional period?

(i) In the 1960s the typical reformer was labeled a *"revisionist"*, and correctly so, I might add. This approach was represented by a coherent group of originally Marxist intellectuals; it still exists at present, but its relative significance has been sharply declining and its Marxist connections have been loosened. This form of thinking is connected with attempts to improve the performance of a centrally planned economy (and society) by introducing particular elements of the market into it. The typical revisionist does not in principle like the market and wants to use it only as an "instrument of indirect control." It is necessary to stress that he considers it to be *an instrument of his control.* He dreams about a "third way," in which the market can be sometimes "used," sometimes "not used." The follower of this approach can be very noisy and very critical, he can successfully demonstrate several visible faults of the system of centralized economic planning and administration of the whole economy from the center but he considers the market to be an overcome, obsolete and inefficient economic coordination mechanism (especially in an era of computers and of the information revolution).

The ever-increasing role of the government is for him a natural and undeniable result of historical evolution. In his argumentation, he often refers to such Western authors as Galbraith, Bell, and even Keynes and similar interventionists. In the 1960s this approach was based explicitly, in the 1980s only implicitly, on Marxism.

(ii) Very strong and uncompromising criticism of the existing system comes from the believers in genuine Marxism, from what I would call *Marxist fundamentalism*. At present, this is such a small group of intellectuals that it can be termed an "endangered species" in this part of the world. Whereas "revisionists" could be found both in the official structures and among leading dissidents in the past, Marxist "fundamentalists" lived and live at the periphery of society. They disdain the economic dimension of life (both for themselves and for the "masses"), and are interested in ideology and in the perfection of mankind. The existing system is for them nothing more than a new version of "state capitalism."

(iii) Whereas Marxist fundamentalism is an elitist movement and is confined to a very small circle of intellectuals, *antibureaucratism* is a popular (and populist) criticism of everyone who is of the white collar class. This approach has a very long tradition in this country (the experience of the Austro-Hungarian empire) and its adherents usually do not criticize the system, but rather particular people in it. An officially sanctioned criticism of bureaucrats, which has become a specifically Czech behavioral pattern, well known in the famous figure of "brave soldier" Svejk, represented an extremely unproductive and nihilistic approach that efficiently blocked any far-reaching social change.

(iv) The very loud and very self-confident *technocrats* see the world in technical or engineering terms and believe in an inevitable "inertia of progress." They are, therefore, surprised that this is not in fact happening in their own country. They see their own colleagues in Western countries and compare their living standards and professional opportunities with their own. Their criticism of the government's evident failure—basically they interpret it as the incompetence of the existing government—is based on a totally false conception of what a good government ought to do. They do not understand the role of the invisible hand in human progress and attempt to design an alternative system with a better and more competent government. "Because of their belief in the superiority of "expert" knowledge, they find it difficult to understand "systematic" explanations for social events and hence view the social world as a consciously designed system open to modification and "improvement" by those selfsame intellectuals."[1]

Genuine criticism of the current social and economic order—based on such, often mutually conflicting, ideas—can help to create an atmosphere of general discontent and dissatisfaction as well as the feeling that it is necessary to introduce significant changes very quickly. Yet the nontrivial problem remains: can such criticism constitute the basis for a successful strategy for the transformation of the present system or does it—by concentrating attention on wrong targets—help to preserve the existing system and lead reform activity in the wrong direction?

---

[1] Sowell [1980].

II. Digression on the Interpretation of the Mode of Operation of the Original, Nonreformed, Economic System in Eastern Europe

A feasible reform strategy relies heavily on the starting conditions in the reforming countries, as regards both their economic situation and their economic system. Because many misunderstandings exist in this respect, I would like to argue that the past, very complicated economic system in Eastern Europe, which was based on a mixture of vertical and horizontal economic relations, on hierarchies on the one hand and on extremely distorted, and therefore inefficient markets on the other, was, nevertheless, very different from the textbook model of a centrally planned economy (both in Eastern and Western textbooks). This has been very often overlooked.

The inefficient, wasteful and environmentally damaging economy (as in Czechoslovakia) was and is a fuzzy and unstable mixture of vertical and horizontal relations between the government on the one hand and firms and households on the other, and of horizontal relations among firms, among households, and between firms and households. The textbook model of a centrally planned economy, which emphasizes commands (directives) originating from omnipotent and extremely powerful (originally, decades ago), and less omnipotent and less domineering (in the recent past), central planners to the obediently behaving (initially) and more independent (at present) firms, may be a useful first approximation or a good educational device for freshmen, but it is a misleading concept for a realistic understanding of the main ingredients of the prereform system.

The standard interpretation, shared both by Western sovietologists and by many domestic reform economists, was, and is, dominated by the strong impression made by the undeniable existence of institutional arrangements, by the Central Planning Board, by the monobank, by the annually repeated planning ritual, etc. This interpretation, however, neglects the importance of several incremental changes that have been brought about through a long evolution that began soon after the introduction of central planning.

The historical and evolutionary interplay of interests, ideology, and institutional structures has created a very specific economic system, one which can be described by the following "stylized" characteristics:

(i) It is not correct to call many highly diversified forms of government intervention into the economy "planning." We were, in reality, witnesses of arbitrary, ad hoc, and incoherent interventions.

(ii) The government was not (and is not) a single unit: it was a sum of competing interests of individuals (or various groups) inside and outside the "center," and the logic of the system "favored socially counterproductive pursuits of narrow personal goals."[2] This provided short-term benefits to a small number of special interests at great costs to the rest of society.

(iii) Because of the extremely powerful monopolistic and rent-seeking firms, the central authorities were in effect deprived of the tools of both governing and ruling. Kornai [1980] is correct in his Economics of Shortage when he writes that "not even in the strictest periods of centralization was the plan directive a one-sided dictate," and in our analytical works we stressed bargaining between planners and "planned" firms or even an "upside-down

---

[2] Sowell [1980].

pyramid" of decision-making in a so-called centrally planned economy. [3]

(iv) Even if Posner [1987] may have a point in his statement that "the distinction between market and non-market economies may be as arbitrary as it is misleading," I agree with Friedman [1984] when he argues that in a socialist economy "it is a very distorted market, but it is a market nonetheless." A market should not be defined as an efficient market, a market should not be identified with an unhampered pricing mechanism; in essence, a market is not the same thing as perfect competition. The East European economies were based on the extremely complicated interaction of economic agents (= a market); and the decision-making of their main micro-economic agents—firms and households—was governed by (properly defined) prices and incomes, similar to a standard market economy.

It is not my intent to develop this argumentation in more detail here. Rather, I would only like to stress for the last two decades the following points:

— Although the role of state has become less domineering, this does not necessarily mean it has become less paternalistic and less counterproductive.

— Prices were not based on the incidental, totally voluntaristic decisions of the bureaucratic apparatus, as it was often claimed. Rather, they were the result of various interacting, countervailing forces, and in this respect were (and are) very "real" and in a sort of "equilibrium." It must, however, be stressed that an economy with such a distribution of power has an extremely inadequate capacity

---

[3]   Mlcoch [1990].

to generate the right (scarcity) prices necessary for rational decision-making and for the efficient allocation of resources.

— I have argued elsewhere that economic disequilibrium (repressed inflation) was, in the past, deliberately introduced into the economy by planners.[4] Their behavior can be characterized by an "aversion to equilibrium." As a public choice school scholar remarks: "by setting prices below the market clearing level, the planners, with the ability to allocate the resulting shortage, can create wealth for themselves."[5] Disequilibrium was, hence, in the deepest personal interest of the planners.

— Markets were imperfect in several respects. Monopolistic defects are often mentioned in the comparative economic literature, but the incompleteness of the market (the existence of vast "unoccupied" territories) and the indefinite boundaries between economic agents (due to the complicated vertical relations) are left almost unnoticed. Both, however, were responsible for a world full of negative externalities that are so dramatically demonstrated by the acute ecological crisis in the whole of Eastern Europe nowadays.

III. Outline of the Reform Strategy

Leading Czechoslovak economists (and politicians) advocate a rapid transition from a centrally planned economy towards a market economy, since they understand that there is no time to wait. In this respect, our

---

4   Klaus, Triska [1988].

5   Levy [1988].

intentions are clear. We definitely do not want to repeat our mistakes of the 1960s, when we attempted to introduce a hybrid system between central planning and market economy—we are not interested in a "third way." As someone recently stated, the third way is the fastest way to the Third World.

We want to achieve the transition from a state-dominated economy to an economy based on private property, private initiative, and private entrepreneurship. We do not intend to orchestrate the economy from above and we do not want to start another vicious circle of pseudo-rationalistic engineering based on ambitions of irresponsible intellectuals and technocrats.

We are increasingly convinced that our country, or any other, is less unique than it is often claimed. There are some specifics, some differences, but there are more similarities, including the basic economic laws that are valid across continents, economic systems, and ideological beliefs. Let me stress the following points:

(i) A partial reform is much worse than a nonreform. This is a message which was explicitly clear from the partial reform in Czechoslovakia in the 1960s. And it is the message we received from carefully studying the reforms carried out in Central and Eastern Europe in the last two decades. A partial reform in a distorted economy is a tremendous and dangerous mistake.

(ii) In favoring a nonpartial and comprehensive reform, I do not intend to wait for an all-embracing reform blueprint. This is, in my opinion, a very important stance, because to wait for an ambitious and intellectually perfect reform project that is elaborated in all details means to postpone the reform to eternity. Even worse, since reform has already begun, to wait for a blueprint now would very quickly lead to a chaotic disintegration of the economy, similar to what we see nowadays in the Soviet Union. To wait is one way of falling into "the reform trap."

(iii) A reform project means a plan for several crucial reform steps in a proper sequence. A reform project does not mean that we understand all the details; that we know in advance all the steps; that we have all the data for all possible scenarios. (I often compare the transformation process with playing chess. In order to play chess, one must know the rules, and one must know the basic opening strategies. But it is not possible to know the situation on the chessboard after the 15th or 25th move).

(iv) Traditional economic reform in the East, known for decades, is, as we call it, a trap. It is a trap for at least two reasons. One is connected with the micro-aspect of the problem and the other with the macro-aspect. We understand that the traditional reform paradigm of "decentralization" is a dangerous mistake unless it is accompanied by fundamental changes in the existing pattern of ownership. And this has not been the case so far in any reforming centrally planned economy. As long as the state remains the ultimate owner of assets, it will always in the last resort "save" the loss-making enterprises from bankruptcy. As experience teaches us (particularly in Hungary), bargaining between the enterprises and the central planning authorities about the targets and tasks contained in the state plan is replaced by bargaining about the granting of easy credits and fiscal subsidies from the state financial institutions. Needless to say that in this tug of war, enterprises are most often on the winning side. Another crucial point is the extreme monopolization of the economy, which means that the enterprises are very powerful. It is therefore quite clear that within the prevailing state property, the measures and steps aimed at decentralization of decision-making processes can not suffice to bring about the desired changes in the pattern of behavior of economic agents, particularly of producers. Even if at first the idea of decentralization in an overcentralized economy sounds quite rational, it is in fact a misunderstanding. It is a trap because the decision-making done by the micro-agents brings—ceteris paribus—more problems than solutions.

The second danger is connected with macroeconomic mistakes. Even if the major challenges for the transformation process are microeconomic in nature, sound macroeconomic policy is essential if the reform process is to succeed. Restrictive monetary and fiscal policy is the precondition for any successful economic reform. Without it, we are in the reform trap again.

In this respect, a budget surplus for the year 1990 seems to us a very important precondition for the success of the whole reform process, for the success of all other aspects of the reform. At the same time, we have implemented a very restrictive monetary policy with the target zero rate of growth of money supply.

(v) Another major obstacle to a successful economic transformation is the lack of transparency of basic economic relations in a post-centrally planned economy. All economic agents at the microlevel, the government, as well as the architects of the reform, are in reality blind because of the lack of transparency in two areas: in the field of property rights and in the field of prices. We have understood that the early rapid transformation of property rights is absolutely crucial for the reform to succeed.

When the disassembly of central planning occurs, we are witnesses of a chaotic, extremely inefficient, and extremely unjust privatization regardless of the intentions of politicians or the architects of the reform. There is thus no time to wait.

Under the Ministry of Finance, we have established a special board, called the Board for the Temporary Administration of State Property and Its Privatization. This board has already prepared the basic concept of the privatization scheme.

Our project has two standard stages. The first stage is the commercialization of the existing state firms, their transformation into what we call "the privatizable form," which means the formation of joint stock companies (with shares in the hands of the government) in the crucial part of the Czechoslovak economy. In the second stage (actual privatization), the shares will be sold to the public by the means of auctions. This is a standard procedure. The obvious questions that remain are *who* the private investors will be, *how much* will be offered for sale and *for what price*. We have one specific way of realizing this stage. Because of the lack of domestic capital, it will be necessary to augment the wealth of the population by distributing freely a part of state property in the form of vouchers to the population at large. And only at the next stage will it be possible to start the exchange of vouchers for the shares of the state joint stock companies.

The very early transformation of the property rights, merely to prevent the chaotic privatization that is presently occurring, is absolutely essential. There is no time to privatize five percent of the state property in two, ten, fifteen years, as was done in some developed and developing countries in the past decade. We must start with the bulk of enterprises and privatize them in a few months' time. No other possibility is viable.

Relative prices must be changed at the early stage of the reform process, too. We understood that only a very small part of the price restructuring can be achieved in the form of a centrally orchestrated price correction or price rectification; most of it must be done, and will be done, by the invisible hand of the market after the price liberalization that we plan to introduce at the beginning of 1991.

In the past we have assumed that a greater share of the price correction would be done by an administratively orchestrated action. But we are discovering more and more that there are only few price changes that are transparent enough to be brought about by the center. We now realize that this intermediate corrective step will be much smaller than we expected.

In this respect, however, there are several questions and doubts. We are quite certain about the sequencing between price liberalization and restrictive macropolicy. But we are not as certain about the proper sequencing as regards the improvement of the quality of the market (and the market structure) on the one hand, and price liberalization on the other. Should we start with the "nurturing of the market" or with price liberalization? I must admit that at the beginning we stressed the role of "nurturing the market structure" as a precondition for price liberalization, but I am now less certain about this choice since under rigid prices the market cannot be "nurtured."

We are also not sure about the sequencing with regard to the institutional restructuring at the microlevel and the liberalization of prices. It is quite clear that it would be counterproductive to adjust and liberalize prices before economic agents have the incentives and sufficient freedom to respond. Yet, at the same time, we realize that markets are unlikely to function effectively without an appropriate degree of price flexibility.

Finally, sequencing with regard to domestic institutional and price measures on the one hand, and liberalization of foreign trade and the rate of exchange on the other, is another problem. It is evident that the flexibility of exchange rate movements and convertibility must be established at a relatively early stage of the reform process, and we hope to achieve this by the end of 1990 (because the current exchange rate makes the removal of import controls impossible) together with price liberalization. But institutional changes will take a much longer time.

Such questions are very pragmatic. We do not know whether we can expect a rapid, or whether we can expect a positive supply response to the set of drastic reform measures we are introducing. Nor do we know how rapid or how positive such a response could be. There are first signals of output losses, of some decline in industrial output, of some acceleration of prices, etc. I do not want to dramatize the situation, but what the supply response will be in the short term is a big unknown.

Also important in this respect is an enormous problem that I stress in spite of all my liberal rhetoric. I do not know how to minimize the ability of some individuals to reap the enormous rents that will become available in the existing distorted system once central controls are lifted.

My interpretation of the reform problem suggests that there is no other way to solve this question than by a pragmatic approach. In my understanding, true liberalism considers the promotion, not the organization of social reforms as its main task. As a believer in this concept I do not pretend to know all the solutions; in fact, I consider one of my primary tasks to be to block faulty political decisions. Reform in a "rent-seeking environment"—as Tollison reminds us is a very dangerous social speculation and undertaking, and we cannot afford to put our fates once again (after forty years) into the hands of irresponsible intellectuals.

References

FRIEDMAN, Milton, Alec NOVE, *Market or Plan? An Exposition of the Case for the Market*. Centre for Research into Communist Economies, Occasional Paper, No. 1. London 1984.

KLAUS, Václav, "Socialist Economies, Economic Reforms and Economists". In: *Communist Economies*, No. 1, 1989.

——, "Monetary Policy in Czechoslovakia and the Nature and Problems of the Current Economic Reform". In: *Communist Economies*, No. 1, 1990.

——, Dusan TRISKA, "Ekonomické centrum, prestavba a rovnováha". In: *Politická ekonomie*, No. 8, 1988. (English version, "Economic Center, Reform and Equilibrium". In: *Czechoslovak Economic Digest*, No. 2, 1989).

KORNAI, Janos, *Economics of Shortage*. Amsterdam 1980.

LEVY, D., The Bias in Central Planned Prices, Center for the Study of Public Choice, George Mason University, Working Paper, 1988.

MLCOCH, L., "Chování cs. podnikové sféry (The Behavior of Czechoslovak Firms)". In: *Ekonomicky ústav CSAV*, 1990.

POSNER, Richard A., "The Law and Economics Movement". In: *American Economic Review*, Vol. 77, No. 2, 1987, pp. 1-13.

SOWELL, Thomas, *Knowledge and Decisions*. New York 1980.

Karol Lutkowski

The Polish Program of Stabilization

I. Introduction

On January 1, 1990, Poland embarked upon a radical program of monetary stabilization and institutional change, designed to transform its economic system into an authentic Western-style market economy. The program made possible by the profound transformation of the internal and external political situation of the country is to be viewed as an attempt to address the deep-rooted systematic causes of disequilibrium and inefficiency in the economy and, at the same time, as an essential support to the nation's effort to change its political system into a parliamentarian democracy. Its contents and the general order of economic priorities have been endorsed by the IMF and the World Bank as well as by numerous representatives of the Western creditor countries, although its adoption has been subject to a sovereign decision of the new, democratically elected Polish government and of the Parliament. To strengthen the country's finances, the IMF offered a credit of 746 million dollars, with the World Bank pledging financial support to the amount of 2.5 billion dollars for the coming three years. The move to "domestic" convertibility of the Polish zloty has been supported by a "stabilization fund" of one billion dollars put at the disposal of Poland by the OECD countries.[1] Together with bilateral assistance from various sources, that brought the overall official financial assistance

---

[1] 300 million dollars in grants plus 700 million dollars in credit.

offered Poland at the inception of the stabilization program to the sum of approximately 5 billion dollars. In addition to that, a more forthcoming attitude of Western creditors in rescheduling debt commitments of the country was certainly a significant new element even though a more fundamental solution to the problem of Poland's external hard currency indebtedness of 40 billion dollars remains an open issue. However, it was clear from the outset that the formidable dimensions of the challenge and the inevitable harshness of the program made the whole venture crucially dependent upon the population's willingness to support the government's efforts and to put up with the ensuing hardships. Although the social costs of the stabilization program in terms of decline in real incomes has been twice as great as originally expected (roughly 30 percent), and in spite of occasional sociopolitical strains (e. g., railway strikes and farmers' protests) that understanding and patience have until now been displayed to a remarkable degree, as noted by numerous foreign observers.

Having decided upon the mix of measures to be taken, the basic question that the government had to face was the problem of the time sequence and of the speed of action. That question remains controversial even now, with some critics arguing that the path actually chosen was not the optimal one and that the "shock" approach unnecessarily increased the social cost of the reform. However, it should be pointed out that the country was clearly in a hyperinflationary situation in late 1989, with the rate of growth of the price level in the range of 30-40 percent per month in the last quarter.[2] There was a very serious danger of complete monetary disarray in the near future

---

[2] Although the rate of inflation in 1989, as a whole, was 600 percent.

and action had to be taken swiftly if total economic collapse was to be avoided. The former (communist) government completely lost control over the budget in mid-year and the vicious circle of inflationary spiralling was unwinding with even greater speed. Thus, absolute priority was given to halting inflation even before any serious demonopolization and restructuring effort could have been made. Second, historical evidence on fighting hyperinflation seemed to indicate that "shock treatment" stood a better chance of success and, on the whole, promised to be less costly in terms of social hardships and output lost than alternative, more "gradualistic" approaches. Those considerations were an important factor in determining the strategy chosen, namely, stopping inflation first and doing it swiftly, while preparing—as fast as possible—the necessary groundwork for more fundamental institutional and systematic changes in the future. Demonopolization, privatization with restructuring as well as creating appropriate institutional infrastructures for the capital and labor markets had to be postponed till the moment when the basic monetary framework for stability has been put in place. That exposed the government's strategy in the eyes of some critics to the charge of having an excessive "monetarist" slant. It seems to me, however, that the strategy was thrust upon the government by circumstances rather than being the outcome of a conscious espousal of a particular doctrinal position.

II. The Design of the Stabilization Program

The most essential elements of the program consisted in liberalizing the prices, abolishing all quantitative restrictions on imports, introducing a more uniform tariff congruent with the GATT principles, abolishing fiscal privileges and drastically reducing budget subsidies. The budget was to be brought into equilibrium by a sharp reduction of the government's expenditures, and firm control over the supply of money by the bank system was to be immediately imposed. In addition to the above mentioned measures aiming at laying the groundwork for the freely operating market mechanism and establishing the fundamental conditions of economic equilibrium, the program was provided with two critically important "anchors" of stability: a stable and uniform rate of exchange, at which the Polish zloty became "internally" convertible, and a prohibitive tax on above-the-norm wage increases, designed to keep in check the wage dynamics.

The price liberalization has been radical, affecting prices on 90 percent of the GNP. The only prices still subject to control are the prices for coal, electricity, hot water and central heating, house rents, transport services, some pharmaceuticals and pure alcohol. However, the program started with a very steep rise of some of those administered prices, e. g., the price of coal rose by 400 percent and 600 percent (for enterprises and individual consumers, respectively) and the price of electricity was increased by 300 percent in January 1990. The budget subsidies on those important items were thus cut by four-fifths. Further price corrections on those goods and services were left to be effected later in the year. It is also to be noted that controls on prices of oil and petroleum products were abolished. Those drastic measures, though socially painful, permitted the absorption of the monetary overhang in the economy and brought the structure of the price system into greater harmony with economic scarcity relations. In addition to removing price distortions, they made it possible to reduce by half the amount of subsidies, which constituted more than 30 percent of the total budgetary expenditures in 1989.

Opening of the hitherto closed internal market to foreign competition was from the outset considered to be one of the most important elements of the new economic program, both for short-term and long-term reasons. While introducing convertibility of the zloty on current account, all quantitative restrictions were abolished and supplanted by a pretty uniform customs tariff, although some items (e.g., automobiles, consumer electronics, tobacco, some textiles) were made subject to surcharges for a transitional period of unspecific length. Similarly, a number of articles remained subject to export quotas (some food and raw materials) in order to ensure adequate supplies on the home market in the critical period of transition to the market economy and to prevent re-export of raw materials imported from the CMEA bloc. What is particularly important, all income tax priviliges, preferential rates of interest and subsidies have been abolished in the export sphere. It should be noted, however, that custom duties have been subsequently drastically reduced or suspended and some of the initial export quotas have been abolished in the meantime.

The fundamental condition of restoring equilibrium and of successful transition to an open free-market economy was, of course, seen in the re-establishment of the balance in the sphere of public finances. Already in 1989, the new government made determined efforts to reduce the size of the snowballing deficit and managed to bring it down somewhat in the last quarter of the year. The stabilization program includes the commitment to limit the deficit to not more than one percent of GDP, which could be financed by issuing government bonds. Financing the deficit by credit from the central bank is no longer allowed. The structure of the budgetary revenues was to remain more or less unchanged throughout 1990—a major change should come in 1991 with the transition to a completely new tax system, modelled on the West European standards.[3] The main burden of adjustment in the course of stabilization was imposed on the expenditure side of the budget. The chief elements of expenditure reduction—in addition to the items previously mentioned—consisted in dismantling remaining food subsidies and curtailing administrative expenditures of the government. The planned budgetary deficit of one percent of GNP was to be compensated by a surplus of revenues in the so-called extra-budgetary funds,[4] so that the general government finances were expected to remain in an approximate balance by the end of the year. To strengthen control over the expenditures, the release of funds exceeding 75 percent of the sums allotted in the budget for a given purpose was made conditional upon the approval of the minister of finance.

The second pillar of the macroeconomic framework for stability, complementary to the balanced budget, was to be a tight monetary policy. The task ascribed to it consisted in securing positive real interest rates and in drastically curtailing the rate of growth of the quantity of money to the level consistent with the projected path of the price level. The basic assumption of the stabilization program was that after the initial jump of prices by approximately 45 percent in January, the rate of inflation will steadily decline and that approximate stability of the price level will be reached in the second semester, with the general price level at the end of the year being almost twice as high as

---

[3] Including VAT and personal income tax.

[4] A remnant of the old system, progressively being reduced.

at the beginning. In view of the preceding tendency to a "parallel currency" system (with the dollar component constituting 60 percent of the overall money supply at the end of 1989) the primary aim of the monetary policy in the initial phase of stabilization consisted in restoring confidence in the zloty and making zloty deposits relatively more attractive than dollar deposits. Simultaneously, flexible interest rate policy was to serve as a bulwark for preserving convertibility at a stable rate of exchange. The autonomy of the central bank was confirmed by law. The central bank was charged with the task of restoring and safeguarding the stability of the national currency by means of instruments, mainly of the market-type character, which it should further develop and refine.[5] In view of the technical difficulties of implementing the policy of flexible rates of interest within the framework of the institutional underdevelopment of the two-tier banking system, it was decided to fix the basic rate of refinance credit and deposit rates on a monthly basis for a time. The old-type credit planning and credit quotas were discarded, even though—incidentally—it may be argued that a modified version of quantitative targeting could be useful in the present situation.

The far-reaching changes in the sphere of foreign exchange policy were probably the most daring and innovative element of the program. The essence of the changes in that field consisted in introducing a uniform and stable exchange rate and making the national currency convertible in a single move (for current transaction

---

[5] Interest rate on refinance credit, minimum reserve requirements and—at a more advanced stage of development of the instrumentarium—the open market operations.

purposes). The leap into convertibility was preceded by a series of devaluations of the zloty in the course of 1989. In the process, the value of the dollar in terms of zloty was raised from 512 zloty at the beginning to 6500 zloty at the end of 1989, which means a rise to a level 12 times higher than at the outset (while prices rose to a level that was 6 times higher). On announcing convertibility, effective since January 1, 1990, the price of the dollar was raised sharply once again from 6500 zloty to 9500 zloty, which is the level at which it has been maintained ever since. Formally, Poland has a dual-rate of exchange system because the rate of exchange on the parallel market is free to move.

In practice, however, the divergence between the two rates is being monitored very closely by the central bank, which is ready to take appropriate action either by intervening or by modifying the rate of interest in order to smooth out excessive differences. In practice, therefore, the rate has remained uniform and stable up to now (until mid-1990). It must be added that capital transactions are subject to controls for the time being: the flow of investments and the transfer of profits are regulated by separate legislation (now under review), and private transfers abroad are limited to 500 dollars, without license, per traveller. However, foreign money may be drawn from foreign-exchange accounts held with the Polish banks without any restrictions. Otherwise, capital transactions with the outside world and holding bank accounts abroad are subject to a system of permits (general or individual in character). Notwithstanding those reservations, the introduction of domestic convertibility was considered a very important qualitative change in the economic system and—being implemented at the height of the economic crisis—was generally judged to be the most risky element of reform.

Finally, it was believed impossible to break the hyperinflation spiral and to retain a stable rate of exchange without a firm check on the growth of money wages. The method selected consisted in suppressing wage growth in excess of the norm by means of a prohibitive tax (ranging from 200 to 500 percent of the total excess payments). The norm itself was determined by a set of sharply restrictive coefficients of compensation for inflation—0.3 for January, 0.2 for February, March and April, and 0.6 and more for the later months.

The implementation of the program of stabilization was to extend to the whole of 1990, although the main effort of rooting out inflation was to be accomplished in the first half of the year.

III. Provisional Results of the Polish Stabilization Program

The first half of the year of the implementation of the present stabilization program brought a number of surprising results, both positive and negative. Remarkable improvements were noted in the sphere of macrofinancial indicators of the economic situation of the country; namely, the monthly rates of inflation, the budgetary balance, the development of the basic monetary aggregates, the balance of payments, the dynamics of foreign exchange reserves and the behavior of the rate of exchange in the entirely new situation of free convertibility. Negative side effects took the form of a much higher than expected initial jump in the level of prices following the transition to free-market pricing, a sharper decline in the level of real wages, then—with a delay—a deeper recession in the production sphere[6] and unexpectedly slow progress in the restructuring of production. Structural rigidities, deeply rooted cost inefficiency, accustomed ways of management behavior as well as monopolistic vested interests and entrenched positions proved to be a tougher challenge than many had assumed. Fast progress in the macroeconomic sphere was not matched by equally rapid progress at the microlevel. Numerous enterprises retrenched, pushing up prices as high as possible and curtailing production instead of trying to adapt flexibly to changed conditions. Complaints and protests about the unexpected "demand barrier" became a regular feature of press and TV interviews with representatives of industrial management and labor. It was only slowly that a serious effort of searching for alternative outlets and sources of supply developed, and after the first few months, export activity began to display unexpectedly strong dynamics.[7]

At first, the public was shocked by the sudden rise in prices, at the rate of 76 percent in January alone. Subsequently, the rates of inflation began to decline to ever-lower levels reaching single digits (4 percent in April, 5.5 percent in May and an estimated 3 percent in June).

According to current estimates, in the second half of the year, inflation will be reduced to 1–2 percent per month.[8]

Probably the greatest positive surprise, and the most visible sign of the return to stability, was the behavior of

---

[6] All the afore-going indicators were approximately twice as high as originally assumed.

[7] Though still without clear signs of energetic pro-export restructuring in the pattern of production.

[8] Apart from the probable upsurge in July as a result of drastic cuts in the remaining subsidies.

the rate of exchange and of the freely operating foreign exchange market. Up to now, the experiment of convertibility has proven to be an unqualified success: the free market (parallel) rate of the zloty remains closely aligned with the official rate and shows signs of enduring strength, at least at the moment (mid-1990). Instead of the projected 800 million dollar deficit on current account, it now seems that the country will earn a relatively sizable surplus over the year as a whole. Export is developing fast and over the first half year foreign exchange reserves have grown.

It should be noted, however, that the present relatively strong position in the balance of trade is largely due to recession. The trend may be easily reversed when the level of economic activity picks up again. The rise in foreign exchange reserves by 2.5 billion dollars in six months was only partially due to the trade surplus and the current account overall surplus of 1.2 billion dollars. The greater part of the growth in reserves was due to the very tight monetary policy, which forced many economic units to convert foreign currency in their possession into Polish zlotys. The extremely tough stance of the monetary policy is slowly being somewhat relaxed. It is expected, however, that there will be no major U-turn in policy, as that might put at risk the gains in monetary stabilization already achieved.

The growth of the money supply in nominal terms over the first half year have remained within the assumed limits, although the sharp jump in prices at the beginning of the year (132 percent over the first quarter) reduced the real value of the money stock at the end of the first quarter by half, in comparison to December 1989. It has started to grow slowly since then. An important achievement of the monetary policy—at least in the opinion of most experts—

consisted in the eventual establishment of the positive real rate of interest. Apart from January, when the rate of interest turned out to be less than half of the actual rate of inflation,[9] it soon approached closely the appropriate, i.e., positive and real, level and since April it has been marginally higher than the rate of inflation. Since July 1, 1990, it is being determined on the annual basis again. In view of the expected further decline of inflation, it has been set at 34 percent per year and will be modified in the light of future experience. One interesting aspect of the monetary policy under entirely new conditions may be noted in passing: contrary to expectations, the greater part of the additional money creation was provided by the growth of foreign exchange reserves and not by domestic asset creation by the banking system. In that sense, it may be argued that the Polish central bank, rather untypically, has "over-performed" the task, which had both positive (long-term) and negative (short-term) effects on the overall performance of the economy in the first phase of stabilization. Although some critics maintained that the credit squeeze has been excessive and has contributed to deepening the recession, it must be pointed out, too, that the inflation has not been completely squeezed out as yet and remains a very real danger.

The same ambigous (both critical and positive) assessment may be levied, I think, at the budgetary policy. Instead of the expected deficit, equivalent to one percent of the GNP on the annual basis, the budget for the first half of 1990 has been closed with a surplus of 1.5 percent of the GNP. However, it must be pointed out that the

---

[9] The rate of refinance credit was set then at 36 percent per month.

revenues were fed by unexpected incomes carried over from the past year and one-time windfall financial gains on the sharp devaluation of the currency. Besides it is again possible to argue, in view of the uncertainty reigning at the outset, that it was proper and, on the whole, useful to err on the side of monetary virtue, especially in the light of the financial excesses of the past, rather than to risk endangering the program at the very beginning. In that case there are indications, too, that the situation in the second half of the year will be less favorable to equilibrium and the additional room for maneuver may be extremely welcome. In any case, the public sector was able to diminish its indebtedness toward the banking system by a corresponding amount.

The tax-based wage policy "anchor" has also withstood the pressure under the norms, because of liquidity shortage in many branches of industry and internal trade. However, in view of the "corrective" decline in the value of the zloty, the average level of real wages fell by about 30 percent. The sharpness of the tax brake on wages will now be slightly relaxed, although within the bounds of what is considered to be safe.

It must be admitted that the economic and social costs of the stabilization effort have been heavy up to now. In mid-1990, the economy is stuck in a recession, at a level of production 30 percent lower (judging by the volume of sales) than in the corresponding period of 1989. Unemployment, though still at the level of 3.5 percent of the labor force, may soon grow fast. Some vital sectors, like the food economy and small business have been hit particularly painfully and are now demanding special relief programs. Housing, social services and culture belong to the spheres of social life where urgent financial support of the state is demanded particularly vigorously. Clearly, the point has been reached at which a modified approach to some aspects of the strategy is needed, although the gains achieved so far in the sphere of financial stabilization should not be put in jeopardy.

IV. Concluding Remarks

The present Polish government seems to oppose easy recipes for revitalizing the economy by a general relaxation of the financial policy, being conscious of the dangers inherent in that approach. The Polish economy has probably reached the point at which most stabilization attempts in the recent past got derailed precisely as a result of premature relaxation of the overall stance of economic policy. However, a package of measures has been announced by the deputy prime minister responsible for the reform, Mr. Balcerowicz, which foresees a number of supply-side measures designed to stimulate the productive activity and to support the most endangered areas of social life. The package includes a number of far-going fiscal stimuli to establishing new businesses, the suspension of custom duties on imports of a large variety of inputs, and the allotment of additional funds to housing and agriculture. A thoroughgoing revision of the legislation on foreign investment should abolish administrative obstacles and liberalize the transfer of profits. The central bank is prepared to conduct the monetary policy in a more flexible, though firm, manner.

The present paper has focused attention on the stabilization program alone. It is important to remember, however, that the program is merely the introductory phase of a broader long-range project of profound institutional reform, including the blueprint for a radical change in the structure of ownership of the capital stock, capital market promotion, and expansion and modernization of the financial sector to stimulate the restructuring and growth of the Polish economy. The process of institutional change has already begun. Nevertheless, the country is now on the critical threshold, just before making a decisive move along that road, as the Parliament is debating over the final draft of the privatization bill. Speeding up the process of institutional change, if successfully implemented, could provide a decisive impetus to growth with stability. That is, at least, the implicit assumption of the guiding philosophy of the reform.

V. Summary

The new stabilization program in Poland, initiated on January 1, 1990, is the introductory part of a long-range program of institutional and policy reform designed to transform the economic system of the country into a full-blown market economy. Its overriding concern is to halt inflation and to put the country on the track of stable growth and openness. The basic components of the program are: complete price liberalization, a balanced budget and firm control over the money supply, domestic convertibility of the currency at a uniform and stable rate of exchange and a tax-based wage policy. The results achieved in the first half year suggest a picture of remarkable success in the macrofinancial sphere—a sharp reduction of the rate of inflation, a stable exchange rate and improvement in the trade balance, a positive real rate of interest and the consolidation of public finances—coupled with serious problems in the real sphere. The social and economic costs of monetary stabilization have been high: the reduction of real wages by 30 percent, a sharp decline in the level of production, the absence of a visible movement toward the restructuring of production, growing—though still small—unemployment, and increasing strains in vital areas of social life. It is expected that a recently announced package of supply-side measures and a speeding up of the process of institutional change will help break the deadlock.

Tamás Bauer

Experiences and Prospects: The Case of Hungary

I. Introduction

In this paper, I focus on the present state of economic reform in Hungary. Let me correct myself immediately: while for more than a third of a century we have been speaking about economic reform in Hungary, we are now abandoning this term in favor of transition from a planned economy to a market economy. The difference between these two approaches will be presented in section 2 of the paper. In section 3, the achievements in creating the framework for a market economy will be outlined. In section 4, attention is drawn to some new developments in the actual operation of the system. The most important missing elements of a market economy will be identified and ways to fill in these spaces will be considered in section 5.

II. Abandoning, instead of Reforming, the Planned Economy

Hungary has had experience with economic reforms for more than a third of a century by now. The first reform blueprints were drafted during the mid-1950s, while a comprehensive effort to replace the Soviet-type system of mandatory planning by a unique amalgam of public ownership and national planning with entrepreneurial freedom and market competition was undertaken beginning in 1968 and has not been abandoned since then. The latter issue, namely, Hungary's insistence on this course rather than the undertaking itself, was peculiar in comparison to other countries in Eastern Europe where similar undertakings had taken place several times but were mostly abandoned after the first difficulties in implementation.

The present efforts in Hungary go, however, beyond the objectives of reform policies during the last (more than) two decades. True, the reform blueprint of 1968 already represented a comprehensive effort not comparable with endeavors to "perfect" the planning system in the Soviet Union, Bulgaria, Poland or in the GDR during the 1960s and 1970s. Still, the 1968 blueprint labelled "New Economic Mechanism" by its designers maintained some central features of the traditional system.

The reform blueprint drafted in the late 1960s and maintained, in main points, until the late 1980s has not questioned the dominance of social or, more modestly, nonprivate ownership in the economy. The reformers of the 1960s in Hungary believed that a market economy could operate on the basis of state and cooperative ownership. The reform blueprints did not imply any substantial increase in the share of the private sector in the economy.

During the early and mid-1980s, the stand of Hungarian reformers was somewhat different. The inappropriateness of state ownership in respect of small-scale business, particularly in the service sector, in retail trade, etc., was admitted and the development of private initiative in such sectors was promoted. Thus, the private sector was accepted as an important, indispensable but still subordinate sector in the economy.

The reformers who drafted the reform blueprints of the 1960s rejected the counterposing of plan and market. They argued that plan and market as control mechanisms are not mutually exclusive but coexistent in most modern economies. The reform blueprints implied a far-reaching control of investment and foreign trade by the government. Regional economic development was also to be strongly influenced by government authorities. A mixed price system was to be created where prices are subject to both market conditions and government priorities, and part of them is set bureaucratically by government authorities.

Thus, in the economic system envisaged, market coordination had to play a substantially greater role than in Soviet-type planned economies, while bureaucratic coordination by government authorities had to play a substantially greater role than in Western market economies.

At that time it was assumed that the country would preserve her adherence to CMEA, which would, however, be reformed. When Hungarian economists drafted their reform program during the 1960s, they might have supposed that similar reforms would be undertaken in several other CMEA countries and trade between them would be reorganized on commercial principles. In 1971, the Hungarian government suggested substantial changes in the CMEA system which were, however, rejected then by the vast majority of the member countries. Still, the idea of reducing the role of interstate agreements on deliveries and creating more room for enterprise-level decision making and direct links between enterprises and a bigger role of prices, interests and other financial categories in CMEA trade was preserved and revived during the mid-1980s. This would suggest that the reformed economy operates within the framework of the economic community of market socialist countries.

The reformers of the 1960s in Hungary connected the economic reform with a certain degree of "democratization" of the political system. However, proposals to introduce elements of self-government and pluralism were rejected by party leaderships, even if the proposals did not involve multiparty democracy. Some basic features of the Soviet political system, such as the lack of competing political parties, party control over all social organizations and over the press, the presence of the communist party in workplaces and even the principle of nomenklatura, were not abandoned.

Though much has changed in the official approach to the economic system, the basic features of the 1968 blueprint have been preserved. First, though the reformers allowed some room for private initiative, it was still considered as a minority component of the economy.

Second, the decisive role of CMEA trade and the established mechanisms of CMEA were not questioned. The role of CMEA in the world economy and the contents of its role for Hungary did not change substantially following the price explosions of 1973 and 1975 on Western markets and later on CMEA "markets," but this did not result in a fundamental reconsideration of Hungary's CMEA policy.

Third, nothing changed in the political system during these years.

The dramatic transformation in the Hungarian political scene that followed the May 1988 party conference resulted in substantially new conditions for economic reforms. A multiparty system, free elections and guarantees of civil rights were accepted by the communist party. By the end of the year the communist party had to give up its organizations in workplaces, its militia, most of its property and also the right to have elected a president at presidential elections before the elections to the parliament. By now, the framework of a Western-type parliamentary democracy has been created in Hungary. The Spring 1990 elections deprived the communist party of its government position.

In addition to the new framework for state and party politics, the withdrawal of the communist party from workplaces, the abolishment of nomenklatura, etc., created new conditions for civil life. Freedom of the press has been more or less guaranteed. More essential for us now, the emancipation of the economy from politics is also likely to be accomplished.

In addition to the political conditions, the external economic framework has also changed. By the end of the 1980s, it turned out that the structure characteristic for decades could no longer be maintained. The easily accessible resources of the Soviet Union have, due to the wasteful growth of production both in the USSR and in the countries of Eastern Europe, been exhausted. Thus, the trade between the Soviet Union and Eastern Europe is likely to decline.

At a time when rational calculation is becoming more and more essential everywhere in Eastern Europe and when mutual trade in manufactures is acquiring a greater role in trade within the CMEA, the inappropriateness of the traditional trade system is becoming more and more obvious. The transferable ruble is likely to disappear as trade between more and more CMEA countries is settled in hard currencies. Hungary has already agreed on that with the USSR and Czechoslovakia. Thus, the peculiar mechanisms of trade with CMEA countries which have been an important constraint on business-like behavior of Hungarian enterprises will be eliminated.

III. The Framework for a Market Economy Is Present

The economic system that resulted from the economic reform in 1968 differed from a Western market economy in many substantial respects. Due to the fact that nonprivate ownership prevailed and the private sector was restricted to a secondary role, small-scale business units were missing from the economy. The large state-owned firms formed, together with leading officials of sectoral ministries, strong pressure groups who neglected market impulses. The financial system that allowed for differentiations of tax rates and even numerous exceptions from the rules made a revival of mechanisms of bargaining between government authorities and big firms possible and even likely. The survival of a monobank which is simultaneously a central bank and the only business bank made firms and the bank mutually dependent and prevented the development of a capital market.

During the early and mid-1980s, the Hungarian government did not intend to move from the peculiar Hungarian amalgam towards a Western-type market economy, which might have represented a second comprehensive reform. What they did want, considering the disfunctional effects of these partial aspects of the system, were rather partial changes in all these areas like ownership, taxation, banking, etc. A series of further partial reforms were undertaken during the 1980s, cumulating in the last few years of the decade. As a result, by the end of the 1980s the legal framework for a market economy was created in Hungary.

As a matter of fact, in the negative sense, this was already done during the late 1960s. Mandatory plan instructions and centralized resource allocation were abandoned already at that time. Most of the compulsory associations and trusts that acted as intermediate control agencies between the government and firms were eliminated already at that time, while the rest of them were dissolved during the 1980s. Sectoral ministries were preserved for a time during the late 1960s and 1970s, but they were transformed into one single ministry with fewer powers in industry in 1981. The foreign trade monopoly was gradually abandoned during the 1980s. "Socialist emulation" and the presence of and control by party organizations were abandoned during recent years.

Numerous measures were undertaken to create the framework for a market economy in a positive sense. First, the limitations on private property were gradually lifted. During the early 1980s, new forms of small-scale business were introduced. Leasing of shops and restaurants, etc., to private persons gained ground. "Petty cooperatives" were allowed, often meaning, in fact, private enterprises. The new company law passed in 1989 removed all limitations, since private firms were allowed to employ 500 people. Several legislative acts promoted foreign investments in Hungary.

A banking reform was introduced in 1987: the National Bank turned into a central bank, and five business banks were set up. Half a year later, all firms obtained freedom in choosing banks. In 1988, the new business banks were allowed to extend their activities to collecting deposits from private persons and, in 1990, to foreign exchange operations. In addition to bonds sold to all organizations and persons, the purchase of shares by private persons was also introduced recently.

Although Hungary had a tax system substantially different from the financial systems of centrally planned economies for two decades already, a comprehensive tax reform was undertaken in 1988, bringing the financial system much closer to that of West European countries. A value-added tax and an income tax were introduced. For state enterprises a uniform corporate tax had already existed for two decades; now, a new corporate tax relating both to private and public firms has been introduced. The rates are considerably higher than in most market economies and there are excessive exceptions, but still the tax system follows the principles prevailing in market economies and thus differs fundamentally from the practice of East European planned economies.

This is made possible by the fact that Hungary's prices were adjusted, in many phases, to market criteria. Most of the distortions so familiar in planned economies were eliminated. Relative prices still differ from those in Western Europe but to a much lesser degree than, say in Czechoslovakia. Subsidies were, in most cases, withdrawn or, as in the case of fuels, milk or public transport, considerably reduced.

Domestic prices in Hungary have, during the last two decades, been linked to foreign prices to an increasing degree. A uniform exchange rate has operated for a long time by now. Thus, actual foreign prices affect Hungarian firms' results and they have to rely on them in making decisions.

IV. Changes in the Operation of the System

The substantial changes were not limited to legislation and financial regulation. The process of systematic transformation has already developed quite considerably in many respects during the last two decades.

First, a considerable private sector has emerged in Hungary. The share of self-employed within the active population has now reached 4 to 5 percent. Though this is considerably less than in comparable Western countries (around 10 percent in Austria, Denmark or Finland), it is higher than elsewhere in Eastern Europe. (This figure does not include household plots in agriculture and unregistered activities in the shadow economy.) Hungary has a considerably developed private crafts sector, retail trade sector, road transportation system, and construction industry. In a country where all economic activity was covered by a few hundred big enterprises and another few hundred large cooperatives ten years ago, there are now, in addition to more than one hundred thousand self-employed, thirty thousand new private businesses that are absolutely free of state subsidies and must make profits to survive.

Second, money has become an increasingly effective constraint in the Hungarian economy. Money has been a hard constraint for households for a long time already. While in several neighboring countries households possess money and face serious difficulties in spending it, spending money has not been a problem for Hungarians for many years. True, market supply is not as good as in Western Europe. There is a serious housing shortage, waiting times for new cars are as long as five to six years for types in high demand, and one may be refused a telephone in one's flat for decades. The diversity of industrial goods is less than in the West and, due to instability in supply, forced substitution is frequent. Despite all these shortcomings, for Hungarians it is the lack of money rather than the lack of goods that constrains consumption. Relative retail prices are closer to Western ones than in any other CMEA country (except probably Poland recently).

Third, Hungary has opened her economy vis-à-vis the external world to a higher degree than any other East European country. Hungary has the highest share of foreign trade in national product. More than that, semifinished goods have a higher share in Hungary's trade (both with the East and the West) than in the trade of other East European countries. Thus, Hungary's dependency on foreign trade is not only higher but also stronger (more intensive) than that of other East European countries. Hungarian economists often argue that the Hungarian economy is open only in the statistical sense of the word, while insititutionally it continues to be a closed economy. True, a great deal of trade protectionism is still present in Hungary, but the existence of a uniform exchange rate, the erosion and recently the abandoning of the foreign trade monopoly, and the numerous joint ventures and subsidiaries of foreign companies mean that openness of the economy is part of the everyday experience of Hungarian economic agents.

V. What Remains to Be Done

Despite the market economy framework already created and the above-mentioned developments bringing Hungary closer to a genuine market economy, the economy is still far from being a market economy. Some fundamental differences continue to exist. Three important points need mentioning.

First, state-owned enterprises and large cooperatives operating in a similar way continue to prevail in the economy. They control more than 90 percent of total assets, and the bulk of the social product, and of exports, comes from them. Under such conditions, the behavioral patterns prevailing in the economy are determined by their typical behavior: most private firms "accomodate" to them also. The state firms and the major cooperatives are large, they have excessively large multilevel hierarchies, and their managers are, in respect of their position and behavior, often more similar to officials in a large bureaucracy than to business executives.

Second, the economy is still highly monopolized. The number of agents was dramatically reduced in Hungary during the late 1940s and early 1950s. The reduction continued during the following decades. In many sub-branches, the whole supply was concentrated with one to three suppliers. The entry of thirty thousand new small firms has changed the picture only to a limited degree, since they mostly moved to a few branches (computers, industrial services, wholesale and retail trade, hotels and catering, tourism, etc.) and avoided many others.

Even if, in several branches, the number of suppliers might be sufficient for competition, the lack of an adequate market infrastructure prevents the customer from having a choice between suppliers. Though competitors are present somewhere in the country, they often do not get the chance to get in touch with demand. Therefore genuine competition is rather unfrequent in Hungary.

Third, the lack of a convertible currency means that the opening of the economy towards the external world is incomplete. Firms are not in a position to continuously compare domestic suppliers with foreign ones and sales to domestic customers with exports. Even if import controls are lifted (with respect to two-thirds of Hungarian imports beyond the CMEA area at present), some implicit import controls are unavoidable without a convertible currency, as used to be the case before import controls were imposed during the early 1980s.

Thus, the main tasks in completing the transition towards a market economy are: privatization, demonopolization, creation of a domestic market infrastructure, import liberalization and marketization of trade with present CMEA countries.

Privatization is an extremely difficult issue in Hungary. The experience of Western countries with privatization cannot easily be applied to East European countries. In the West, the governments intend to privatize a limited number of companies (not exceeding a few dozen). In Eastern Europe, hundreds of state enterprises need to be privatized within a few years. In the West, the state-owned enterprises operate in a market environment, on commercial grounds, and thus they have bookkeeping and capital evaluation adequate to a market environment. All this is missing in respect of state enterprises in East European countries. In addition, privatized companies in the West fit into a well-established market economy, while in Eastern Europe the market economy is still in the process of being born. All these factors bring a tremendous uncertainty into the privatization process. Abuses and corruption can hardly be fully avoided, which, in turn, brings about strong negative feelings in the population, feelings that are widely exploited by all political forces rejecting privatization.

Still, privatization is necessary and must be carried out with care and determination. The Hungarian Parliament established a National Property Agency which has to supervise privatization. In my view, a government agency cannot organize privatization itself; the initiative should come from the managers of the firms to be privatized. The National Property Agency must supervise the whole process to avoid abuses.

The social background represents a further problem. Selling out state firms to domestic persons unavoidably leads to a situation in which members of the communist élite who were in the position to "capitalize" their power status during the last decades may turn into capitalists. This process called *uwłaszczenie nomenklatury* (perhaps "impropriation of the nomenklatura") in Poland generates wide social unrest both in Hungary and Poland. In my view, however, this is unavoidable, and the new democracies of Eastern Europe must accept that the members of the communist élite should not be excommunicated from the society in the way the members of the bourgeoisie were forty years ago. Moreover, Hungarian enterprise managers cannot be identified with party officials. A generational change took place in Hungarian managerial strata during the last two decades and many of the managers are primarily experts in their professions and not party cadres. I do not see any sensible arguments for preventing them from participating in privatization.

Demonopolization means, first of all, favorable conditions for entry. This means promoting new small businesses. A vast expansion of small and medium-scale business is required. Favorable conditions for the establishment of hundreds of thousands of new small private firms in the next few years must be created. The most important condition is a favorable economic and political climate. Tax allowances are also needed. In my view, however, the most important condition that is still missing is a market infrastructure that helps small enterprises to have access to imported goods, to modern equipment and to credit. To achieve that, a network of small (essentially private) trading companies (particularly for wholesale and international trade) and small banks is needed.

Commerce is a decisive area. Monopolization is very strong in both foreign trade and domestic wholesale and retail trade. All limitations concerning the setting up and expansion of privately owned commercial firms must be abolished. Joint ventures are particularly welcome in this area. Hungarians (and particularly Poles) have demonstrated in recent years, particularly in the surroundings of Hungarian, German and even Soviet railway stations, how imaginative and initiative they are in this sector. Why not to do this legally, with just a little bit more capital and on a much larger scale? Developing programs to promote new firms in wholesale and international trade seems necessary.

The same holds for banking. The existing business banks are much dependent on the state on the one hand and on their customers on the other. New banks should be established with foreign capital being independent both of Hungarian enterprises and the government.

For a small country like Hungary the liberalization of imports is the most important aspect of the creation of a competitive market. Hungary's serious balance-of-payments problems have hampered the accomplishment of this endeavor. Earlier, during the late 1960s and early 1970s the import of raw materials and equipment was, in fact, free for state enterprises and cooperatives. The fact that much of the state monopoly of foreign trade was preserved at that time and foreign trade companies carried out a certain kind of informal import control made this relatively easy. Even this had to be suspended during the mid-1970s and particularly during the 1980s. Recently, a growing portion of imports has been liberalized. By now, even the remnants of the state monopoly of foreign trade have been eliminated, which limits the possibility of informal import controls.

A full and lasting liberalization would demand a considerable depreciation of the Forint and/or foreign help.

In addition to that, trade with the present CMEA member countries will run on similar lines in the future. Interstate delivery quotas will be abandoned, and Hungarian firms will obtain full freedom in their decisions concerning imports from and exports to East European countries. Payments for deliveries will be settled in hard currencies. This change does not depend on changes in the domestic economic system of the partner countries; it only means that Hungarian firms will have the same rights as Western trade partners of the CMEA countries.

This is the most substantial change in the exter
environment of the Hungarian economy for many decades. It
means that all foreign trade relations will be market
relations. The dependence of firms on government
authorities, the possibility of relying on government
assistance, will be substantially reduced.

Vladimir Zuev

Experiences and Prospects: The Case of the USSR

The Soviet Union is passing through a turbulent period of change with unknown outcomes. People all around the world are eager to learn about the reforms currently under way. They are right when they believe that Perestroika will continue to influence the political and economic order.

In Europe and large parts of the world, much will depend upon what happens in the period of transition. The uncertainties are enhanced by the fact that policies cannot be formulated and anticipated with reference to an established theory of transition from a command economy to a market-oriented economy. There is no such theory. As Dror, an expert on public policy advice and systems reform, has put it, it is not enough to understand a centrally planned economy and a market economy in order to arrive at a concept for the transition from one to the other. [1] The transition is a categorically different problem.

If government policies in established market economies are not very helpful for forming a transition strategy, one may want to consider the experience of other East European countries, which have been in the process of transition for some time, or make use of the experience that West European countries made when they changed from the command system prevailing during World War II to the market economy of the postwar period.

But one must recognize that the USSR is a very special case. The economy is so large that Western assistance can

---

[1] See Dror [1989].

not be as helpful as in the case of other East European countries. Moreover, the "savoir faire" for business management is completely missing. Finally, many peculiarities prevail in the Soviet Union that make the economy untypical.

Let me mention only two of them. One is that large parts of the population are not familiar with the working of the market system and might not easily tolerate the income inequalities that are part of the incentive system. The other deficiency is that the industrial infrastructure is in very poor condition and needs to be completely rebuilt.[2]

I. Experiences

Since 1987 the Communist Party of the Soviet Union has been in favor of a "more market-oriented economy."[3] It is

---

[2] Limitations on the applicability of other countries' experiences were clearly demonstrated during the Soviet-Austrian seminar on the Austrian experiences, organized on April 4-5, 1990, at the Institute of World Economy and International Relations in Moscow with the help of the Austrian National Bank. Such factors, existing in the Austrian case, as inability to use all production capacities after the war, the amount of foreign help and credits in comparison to the size of economy (more than 1.5 billion dollars were received only within the Marshall aid plan, providing for 88 percent of import receipts in, for example, 1944-46)—all those and some other factors are not operational in the case of the Soviet Union.

[3] In June 1987, the Supreme Soviet approved by decree a package of measures concerning the reform of the economic system known as the "Basic Provisions for Fundamentally Reorganizing Economic Management." Ten decrees dealt with the reform of the different elements of
. . .

important to outline this political aspect, although it is not the main subject of this paper. As the CPSU remains the main and most influential party in the USSR, much will depend on its strategy. And the strategy itself is important for the Party to keep its key position in the society. That is why the economic issue lies at the heart of the whole political struggle.

Other parties, now being actively created, are beginning to exert some influence. But the CPSU itself is not homogeneous, either. It embraces completely divergent views about the contents and procedure of reform. With time going on, the economic reform will become even more of a politically sensitive issue. Emerging political pluralism is likely to make the competition between different approaches harder; it may also enhance the risk of a mistake. If the CPSU fails to develop a coherent strategy for reforming the economy, the Presidential Council will assume a much stronger role. In fact, it is through that Council that the President is trying to enforce the reform as he envisages it. The alternative way of pushing the reform within the party and by means of the party seems to be becoming increasingly difficult.

Some important laws have already been adopted. It will be enough to mention legislation (i) on state enterprises,

---

. . .

the system, like Gosplan (State Planning Committee), Gossnab (State Committee for Material and Technical Supply), GKNT (State Committee for Science and Technology), Goskomtrud (State Committee for labor and social problems), finance, banking, statistics, price formation, responsibilities of· regional bodies · and the ministries. But in reality that did not bring significant changes. On the 1st of January 1988, the Law on Enterprises was adopted, in which the autonomy of enterprises was expressed. The New Economic Mechanism was planned to be realized in 1991, when the 13th Five-Year-Plan is to be launched.

giving them more autonomy; (ii) on ownership, providing for the legal status of different forms of ownership; (iii) on cooperatives, enabling them to act like private companies; (iv) on land property, permitting the long-term lease of land; and (v) on the leasing itself, allowing state enterprises to be given to the workforce for lease.

All these developments are steps towards a more market-oriented economy. But they are encountering great difficulties on their way to implementation. Macroeconomic indicators are in a process of deterioration,[4] because some

---

[4] As far as economic indicators are concerned there is a major deterioration in practically all main positions. According to the official statistics (one might guess even a twice as big deterioration in independent unofficial figures), during the first quarter of the current year (1990) the overall volume of industrial production, in comparison with the first quarter of the previous year, has decreased by 1.2 percent. The volume of external trade in current prices shrank by 1.6 percent. The volume of transportation of goods, instead of increasing, was nearly 5 percent lower than in the corresponding period of the year before. 14 percent of industrial enterprises have not fulfilled their obligations for goods deliveries. As a result, consumers received 2.5 billion rubles less worth of products than it was initially expected. Inflation reached 6.5 to 8.0 percent (2.6 percent for basic needs products), is continuing to accelerate, and is expected to reach 21 to 25 percent at the end of the year, if the present tendency develops further. The state budget deficit for a year goes as high as 80–90 billion rubles. Independent sources claim that the money supply during the first quarter of the current year increased by the amount planned for the whole year. The volume of national income during the 1989–1990 two-year period is expected to fall by 10 to 12 percent. It goes without saying that a big part of that deterioration was not directly due to the transition to a more market-oriented economy, but to other factors such as nationalistic disputes, work stoppages, environmental protection preoccupations. Prospects are no better. The estimated decrease in production levels is of no less than

. . .

concrete measures lead to results contrary to those initially envisaged. Here are some examples.

Cooperatives were legally empowered to fix the prices of their products by themselves. This was intended to substantially raise the volume of production, but in reality, the target was never achieved.

Cooperatives were not permitted to be created in the sector of basic industries. Here all major production facilities remained under a system of strict rationing. The process started with the creation of cooperatives, not in addition to state enterprises, but in substitution for them. In fact, monopolistic structures permitted having super profits while keeping the same level of production without any increases. On top of that, cooperatives began to buy state enterprise products at lower prices and to resell them to the population at prices arbitrarily fixed by their own choice of free market prices. Massive speculation lead to a general increase in prices, to empty state shops' shelves and to super profits for cooperatives within the same production levels. The idea was compromised and the authorities were obliged to impose restrictions on the activities of cooperatives.

Another example: Soviet enterprises received the right to deal directly with foreign partners, but their self-finance position was not really introduced. Executives at those enterprises used the operational freedom to sell cheaply the property accumulated with the help of the state-budgetary finance, in order to import consumer goods for their personal use. A rigid system of licensing of exports had to

---

. . .

20 percent in the coming 4 to 5 years. (Izvestia, June 6, 1990).

be established to replace the direct monopoly of the state for foreign trade deals.

These examples show clearly that an initiative, taken separately, might be considered to be appropriate. But when it is launched not in relation to other reform measures, it is doomed to failure. The law on cooperatives cannot work without antitrust legislation, competition policy, etc. External trade reform comes to a halt, or brings a lot of damage, if self-finance principles are not the rule of the game in the industry.

One can imagine that it was difficult to create at once all the legislation needed. And that it could really take a lot of time. But the population did not want to wait any more. So, they decided to consider and adopt laws on a law by law basis. But each new law did not work in the absence of the whole environment. And inevitable drawbacks set the mood of the population against the essence of the legislation, which in itself had developed in general in the right direction. That was the case with the cooperative movement, for example.

A new strategy is being worked out to prepare a package of measures to assure the success of the Perestroika in the economic field. On the 11th of March 1990, the Council of Ministers issued a resolution to prepare the transition to "the economy of plan and market." We will not discuss at the moment the question of whether those two could coexist for a long time and for an unstipulated period, because new structures can not be created in a day and hence the importance of inevitable, peaceful and unharmful coexistence of both. In the Council's resolution a new "package deal" approach is already reflected. A permanent Commission was created under the Presidency of the Head of the Government to work out the program of transition to the "economy of plan and market" in the

USSR, together with drafts of an appropriate legislation. This legislation should comprise a general draft law on the transition to the "economy of plan and market," as well as a whole set of draft-legislative acts and laws concerning employment, prices, the freedom of economic activities, the establishment of enterprises, antitrust policies, foreign investment on USSR territory, taxes on agriculture, the indexation of salaries, and the banking system.

This set should go together with amendments to the Law on State Enterprises and to the Law on Cooperatives. Apart from that, draft resolutions of the Supreme Soviet on the food suppliers' guarantees for the population in "new market" conditions and on social security are expected to be prepared. And on top of all that, quite a number of the Council of Ministers' Resolutions are to be considered, such as an audit, a credit-system reform, rules for the issuing of bonds and shares and the creation of a stock exchange, demonopolization, a single exchange rate, state delivery prices for some agricultural and raw materials products, joint-ventures, and others. The job seems to be enormous. And the Commission is already lagging behind the schedule.

An exceptionally new feature in the economic reform policy is that more reliance is put on Western expertise. That is a clear sign of uncertainty about the measures that should be undertaken and of a deep worry about the necessity of reaching the goal. Abalkin, head of the permanent Committee on Economic Reform within the Council of Minister's structure, was assigned to procure the best foreign expertise in preparing drafts for a transition to a more market-oriented economy. And to prescribe such things in resolutions is quite an unusual matter for the Soviet Union, which reflects both the next to desperate situation and the change in the attitude towards the West (a more gradual one).

It is becoming all the more evident that the "don't know what to do" mood prevails, as after the April 1990 meeting of the Presidential Council the decision on a concrete form of transition to a more market-oriented economy was rescheduled to be taken not before the beginning of 1991. That means, that the governmental program adopted in December 1989 for the development of the economy, which was highly criticized and which was considered to be half dead, continues to go on.

On May 24, 1990, the Soviet Prime Minister Nikolai Ryzhkov made public a report "On the economic situation of the country and on the concept of the transition to a regulated market-economy." The notion of a "regulated market-economy" in itself already signified a step further from a notion of "plan and market" and reflected the reaction to critics of the incompatibility of plan and market as two big concepts in a single economy.

The program fell under severe criticism as soon as it was announced. The biggest issue was price increases. The population began to panic and all the stores were bought out for several days. In fact, the governmental program put the biggest stress on price increases and did not sufficiently elaborate other measures for making the market work. And without these very measures (such as denationalization of ownership) price increases will not help a lot. The government has chosen the easiest way out for itself to redress the state budget deficit. As calculations clearly show, the overall price increase is expected to amount to 200 billion rubles, and measures for compensation envisage paying the population back 135 billion rubles, which makes a difference of 65 billion rubles net price increase at the expense of the population.

What is more worrisome is that this measure is only regarded as one of the prerequisites for the introduction of the market, which still remains in a haze. Price reform, and not necessarily price increases, is really an important prerequisite, but it works only together with the other reforms. And a price rise should follow rather than precede other measures. It so happened, that everybody was suspicious of the government wanting to use the market pretext, not really introducing it, to cover the deficit and to justify another price rise.

Although in the program itself some well-oriented priorities are enlisted—such as real autonomy of enterprises, competition, and budgetary discipline—in reality, while speaking about them, the report uses vague expressions like "it is needed." Nothing concrete in this direction is proposed. But price rises are treated in concrete terms of real steps for their timing. That is what gives the reason for mistrust. A wave of protests arose around the country. That influenced the people's deputies' behavior. The Ukraine, for example, sent a message of concern and rejected the idea proposed by the government, refusing to implement such measures even if they were adopted at Union level. So did Belorussia, Uzbekistan and some others. And the influential newly elected Russian parliament met the transition proposal with strong opposition. All that means that a lot of debate is yet to come before the final approval of the program.

Some of the authors of the program made an appeal to hold a national referendum. But that was rather a speculation, because one can easily imagine that price rises will not be approved by the majority of people. But even without any referendum, a wave of insistence mounted for the government to resign. In a response to that, Abalkin, who is responsible for the reform, said in a meeting at the Institute of Economics at the beginning of June that their intention is first to introduce the reform and then to resign—a strange bit of logic.

The program continued to be discussed at the session of the Soviet Supreme Court of the USSR during the second week of June 1990. The government was insisting on more or less the same version as originally proposed. But big opposition from deputies and the Republics made it highly improbable to introduce the program along the original lines.

Although the necessity of transforming the economy into a market economy was admitted by nearly everybody, at least orally, the understanding of the speed, the means and the measures diverged significantly. By September 1990 the government will have to propose a concrete and more detailed program, and to take into account the modifications proposed. But there is a big probability that alternative programs under elaboration now will compete with the governmental one.

II. Prospects

A lot of people feel insecure about the present situation. There is a natural fear of the free-market instability. That might be one of the most serious problems of continuing with the chosen line. People prefer to live at lower level conditions, but to be 100 percent secure, rather than to take the risk in order to live better. If at the end of 1988 about 40 percent of the population were in favor of the rationing of the food deliveries ("cards-for-food" system), then, at the beginning of 1990, this percentage rose to 58 percent.

It became very popular recently in the Soviet Union to speak about social security for the most vulnerable people—those with low salaries or pensioners. Everybody calms their fears by promising to help them. And as this is really a very sensible subject, not only the government but also the deputies to the Supreme Soviet use this argument to increase their popularity as defenders of the weakest and poorest. It seems that nobody speaks about the people who are in between the "poor" and the well-paid. In the present state of affairs, people in the category of the "average man" will suffer most. But at the same time, they are the biggest hope for Perestroika to relaunch the economy. They are middle-aged, with middle salaries and are potentially the most active. If nobody thinks about them, the drive towards a more market-oriented economy has little chance of success.

Another danger is the nationalistic problem in the Soviet Federation. The disintegration of the Soviet economic complex may do a lot of harm. But at the same time the necessity of rebuilding the economy on the basis of new principles will become all the more acute. This requires speeding up the introduction of new measures and making sure that they really are new. It is interesting to notice the change in the attitude towards the economy, which is now above all being considered to be one of the cornerstones of the new order to save the Soviet Federation. A lot will depend on the behavior of the republics, especially on Russia. The exceptionally new and important "Republic factor" will to a large extent determine the shape and the scope of the economic reform. The influence of this factor will grow.

A great debate is going on whether to apply a shock therapy. People are tired of waiting. They have been waiting for more than seven decades, always being promised a better life in the future. So, the speed of reform is a very hard issue. But, taking into account all present uncertainties about concrete measures for reform, having in mind that we are pioneering new land, and not forgetting social tensions, it would be unacceptably dangerous to use a shock therapy whose results are yet unknown. Even a slight deterioration in the standard of living might already provoke violence.

We have no right to take this high risk under the present circumstances. The stakes are too high. Therefore, I am rather in favor of a gradual approach, but along the whole spectrum of economic life. The fact is that, if tomorrow it is only just a bit better than today, if one more variety of cheese appears on the shelves (if any at all), if the day after tomorrow one more consumer item is freely available, the support of the population will be largely restored. For the time being, the shock-therapy approach, although initially favored, was rejected at the Presidential Council level. But the pressure remains very high.

Gradual change in the economy will contrast with speedy political reforms. That is true. And in fact, the latter might compel the government to act quickly. But experience shows that the economy needs more time to be relaunched to catch up with political change. This is also true in regard to international relations. Quite a lot of achievements have already been made in the fields of human rights, disarmament, and political activities. But economic cooperation between the Soviet Union and Western countries remains practically on the same negligible level. So, it really takes time. But a slight improvement in the internal economy can be shown immediately and afterwards it can be gradually increased.

In the case of the USSR, a reform of the state sector is badly needed. This part of the economy will not be demolished for a long time yet. According to different and the most radical sources, at least 30 percent of the ownership will remain in the hands of the state (the official figure stands at 40 percent). But most of the reformist action is focused upon the creation of the new structures rather than upon giving a new life to the old ones. It may be right to do so. But it is not right to forget about the existing structures.

Some key issues should be outlined. The problem of motivation is at the heart of the whole thing. Wages and salaries never really depended on the productivity and quality of labor. Only that source can provide more goods of a better quality. [5]

Shares for workers and a leasing of state enterprises may also be powerful means of raising interest in producing more and better output. The government is doing a lot now, but as previously mentioned, without a stimulus to increase productivity practically no change occurs, although that might be the most important issue. Sale of shares, land, and other property, as well as leasing, can tie up a lot of hot money, while at the same time giving rise to a new interest to produce. But at the moment, the government is paying more attention to the financial sphere, to the credit system and to monetary reform. It is aiming at reducing the level of money in circulation. But important as this is, it does not necessarily lead to a better motivation to produce.

The lack of goods is the inborn sin of the Soviet economy. Thus, the task is not to reduce the amount of money in circulation by means of freezing wages and salaries or by price increases, as is now the intention, but

---

[5] Motivation could be encouraged by measures going as far as Austria's experiences after World War II, when overtime wages were exempted from taxation in order to stimulate production.

to raise the level of production, and at a faster pace than the increase of money in circulation. Freezing wages and salaries will mean less motivation for producing. Prices will not work without other measures, as we have already seen. Most important at the present conditions is to saturate the market.

Introduction of real competition between economic agents within the economy is one of the most important issues—apparently, more important than price increases, or price reform in general, which might not really lead to higher production levels. Great significance will remain with the cost controlling function of competition.

For example, costs in agriculture in the Soviet Union are very high. An increase in prices for agricultural products will simply justify those high costs and might contribute to the conservation of an inefficient pattern of production in agriculture. At the same time, exorbitant prices have existed officially for a long time within the so-called "agricultural products market system," which is everywhere in the Soviet Union, especially in the larger cities. But the high prices did not contribute to a large extent to production growth in agriculture. Other factors, related to production structures, played a bigger role, factors such as limitations on land property, lack of availability of machinery, fertilizers, other inputs for the agricultural production, etc.

Coming to the question of convertibility, in relation to the subjects already raised in this paper, it is important to note that a devaluation of the ruble and monetary reform can restore temporarily the balance between the amount of money in circulation and the total of prices for goods available (taking into account the speed of their circulation). But that will not be enough for convertibility.

Or at least, it will only be enough for a very short period of time. If the pattern is not changed and if the volume of money continues to grow at a faster pace than production in real terms, then this balance will be easily broken again. Reforms of the credit system in the Soviet Union, playing on the unconditional increase of the amount of credit to get access to, are in fact increasing inflationary pressures and only make it harder to introduce convertibility. For the moment, President Gorbachev's enthusiasm to go faster than initially planned with the introduction of convertibility, expressed at the summit in the USA in June 1990, is not supported by real economic developments in the country.

The strengthening of the private or individual sector will gradually contribute to competition and to an increase in production. It is essential not to destroy or create something artificially. Instead of that, one should establish the conditions for free competition between various forms of ownership themselves. Then the most effective one will naturally prevail.

It is important to avoid extremes. Going to extremes is typical of Soviet history. If all the state's property, all the kolkhoses, are liquidated, it will be no less a disaster than to leave them in peace.

For some period they might prove to be more effective. Let them compete freely. Let us avoid the mistakes of obligatory collectivization from the historical past. Alas, no law on rules of competition is on the table for debate at the moment.

Of course, denationalization is essential. And that is already a priority. It will be done either on a leasing basis, or by issuing shares and selling them to workers. It is interesting to note that the talk about permitting bankruptcies has shifted attention to proposals for transferring loss-making enterprises into the hands of workers. But if only loss-making enterprises are transferred, that will be not a good policy either.

Independence of economic agents is also a focal point. How much freedom of action will be given in practice? The problem of implementation of the legislation has always been the problem in the Soviet Union. Laws on paper might be the best work done, but the lack of an appropriate mechanism for implementation can well decrease the important new legislation to insignificant levels.

There are many proposals now for separating the state budget from the Central Bank's activities in order to avoid offsetting the deficit automatically. But the government opposes any moves towards an independent State Bank. And that gives grounds to doubt the sanity of the state's budgetary policy. The Ministry of Finance is very keen on using taxes to finance the budget, but it is reluctant to impose self-discipline on some of the contestable items of the budget. Thus, the control assumed by new independent bodies, and the increased role of new institutions like the Supreme Soviet, with its numerous commissions, is a very important subject in the present political debate on economic reform.

A question frequently raised is whether the economic reform has a chance of surviving.[6] It can not but survive.

---

[6] A recently declassified (January 1990) NATO report says that Soviet economic reforms will probably fail. The report lists many problems that could afflict the Soviet economic reform program. Among these are:
— a general lack of understanding about finance;
— the lack of monetary instruments to regulate interest rates and credit;
— the lack of basic computer technology for accounting and control in Soviet banks;
— problems in joint ventures with foreign companies,
  . . .

The country has no alternative other than to permit the reform. A lot of reshaping is yet to come. But the drive towards a more market-oriented economy—or I would rather say, towards an economy of free competition between different forms of ownership and different methods of organization of economic life—is inevitable.

One might ask what gives the process of economic reform an irreversible character. We can not find the answer only within the economy. It is directly interrelated with political change, with democracy and pluralism. But pluralism can not be established without an economic basis—that is to say, it should be supported economically by a great multitude of forms of ownership which develop independently of each other. At the same time, this introduction of different forms of ownership cannot be enacted without political change. Democratic support of the market economy is not very evident at the moment. We are thus coming to the point where it is necessary to multiply the natural supporters of the reform. Those might be the people with their own businesses, who take more interest in initiative, and have more at their disposal to support the newly emerging system. Will their number actually increase? The answer will be "yes." And that is the way to more

---

. . .

    including bureaucracy, accounting practice and foreign exchange;
- welfare and subsidy levels that are far too high, although cutting them would probably cause unrest;
- a practice of domestic funding of the budget deficit through bank borrowing that is becoming unmanageable;
- lower economic growth that will cut state revenues in the 1990s.

But my guess is that all of those problems listed above are not completely unmanageable.

142

guarantees of making the process really irreversible within the democratic system.

The country has to use the unique chance of joining the modern democratic and happier part of the world. To achieve this, a huge amount of work needs to be done from the inside and the outside of the Soviet Union. Let us do our best to secure the success of the policy that is opening the door for a better future and that is named Perestroika.

References

DROR, Yehezkel, "Memo for System-Reforming Rulers". In: *Futures*, Vol. 21, pp. 334-343.

IZVESTIA, June 6, 1990.

Heinz-Dieter Haustein

Experiences and Prospects: The Case of the GDR

The command economy seems to be an invention of the Germans, not to count emperor Diocletian's early trials. In the last century the Prussian economist Rodbertus (1805–1875) proposed substituting Arbeitsscheine (labor certificates) for money in order to create a state-socialist order. In the German war economy of 1914–1918, commodity balances were used and in the 1920s the germanophile bolsheviks developed them into the socialist balancing system, the main tool of central planning. After 1945 we reimported this achievement and refined it with the help of computers, only to discover how inefficient this system works.

It broke down under the pressure of declining productivity growth, growing frustration and strain and the sudden peaceful political revolution. The old power structures collapsed like a house of cards (see Figure 1). Now a completely new situation has arisen: the real chance to bring the two Germanies together within a peaceful European development.

Thus the same transition process from a command system to a market economy, envisaged by other countries like Hungary and Poland much earlier, came to us overnight as an immediate concern of our economic life.

The changeover from a command economy to a market economy in the GDR is a very peculiar historic variant: (i) There is urgent pressure for a short transition period, a wide range of parallel measures instead of a long sequence of steps. The reason for this is the exodus of people from East to West (350,000 in 1989, 150,000 in January, February

144

Figure 1: Events in the GDR

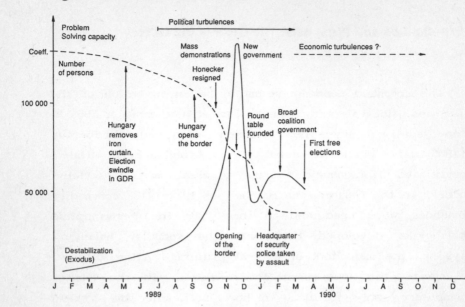

and March 1990), which declined after the first free elections, but can be renewed at any time, if real prospects cannot be ensured. (ii) An immediate currency union between the two German states, which seems imminent, is an extraordinary step for accelerating the transformation of GDR's economy into a market economy. A money constitution is the core of a modern exchange economy. By this "coup de main" an inflation process can be avoided, but there are some other painful results that could lead to a sharp decline of the real income level in the GDR. [1] (iii) A favorable factor is the present economic conditions in the West, especially in the FRG, continuing economic growth and the chances for attracting capital resources for the rejuvenation of GDR's economy. Preparation for the common European

---

[1]   See also Maier [1990].

market opens up new possibilities that can be used in this process.

Table 1: National Economy of the GDR in 1988 in Comparison with the FRG

Indicator	GDR	FRG	FRG=100
Population in mio.	16.7	61.1	27.3
Employees in mio.	8.6	26.1	32.9
GDP* in bn. M/DM	346.0	2118.0	16.3
Growth 1980—88 in % p.a.	4.4	4.6	-
GDP per employee in 1000 M/DM	40.3	81.1	49.7
Fixed Assets 1987 in bn. M/DM	1686.0	8611.0	19.6
Gross Investment in bn. M/DM	77.0	417.0	18.5
Growth 1980—88 in % p.a.	2.0	2.7	-
Gross Wages per month and per employee in M/DM	1269.0	3290.0	38.5
Growth 1980—88 in % p.a.	2.8	3.5	-

*According to Western methodology.

Table 1 shows a comparison of the economic potential of the two German states. Productivity is at a level of 50 percent, capital intensity at a level of 59 percent and wages at 39 percent, as compared to the FRG. In the last years, investment growth and income growth were rather low in the GDR. Table 2 gives an impression of the export performance of the GDR, which is much lower than that of the FRG, even in relative terms. But exports to planned economies are the major part of the GDR's performance and represent existing business contacts, which can be very promising in the future. 443,000 workplaces in the GDR depend upon exports to planned economies. Unification should help our industry to fulfill all existing long-term contracts and to expand these exports together with West

German firms in favorable directions. Structural change is
necessary: a share of 15 percent in exports of raw
materials, energy and metals is an indicator of down-
grading, resulting from the central planning system (see
Table 2 and Figure 2).

Table 2: Export Structure of the GDR Economy in 1988

Indicator	GDR	FRG	FRG=100
Export in bn. VM/DM			
total	90.2	567.80	15.9
for planned economies	62.7	25.00	250.8
for market economies	27.5	542.80	5.1
Machinery, equipment in %	47.6	54.80	-
Consumer goods in %	16.4	12.40	-
Raw materials, energy,			
metals in %	15.1	8.50	-
Intermediate and food			
products in %	7.0	5.50	-
Chemical products, con-			
struction materials in %	13.9	18.80	-
Mutual exports total			
in DM/kg	0.5	1.58	31.6
Electrotechnical goods			
in DM/kg	5.8	37.48	15.5

VM: accounting marks (Verrechnungsmark)

The present (May 1990) situation in the GDR's economy
is characterized by a continuing meltdown of motivation,
which can be measured by the number of people going to
West Germany. The recent proposal of the Bundesbank to
convert wages and salaries at an exchange rate of 2 Marks
for 1 D-Mark brought about a new wave of fear and
mistrust. But on the other hand there are first signs of
recovery and restabilization. The human factor is decisive.
One reason for the exodus is the enormous gap between the
living standards in the two Germanies. (See Table 3)

Figure 2: Price Situation in Metal-Working Industry

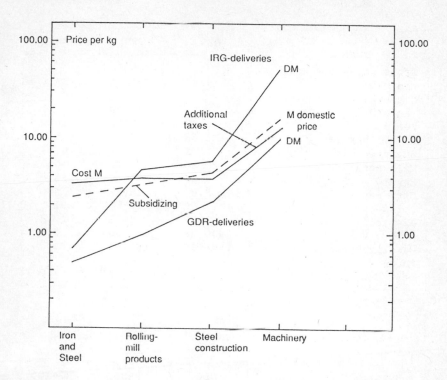

Hourly wages in the GDR are even lower than could be expected by the productivity gap. When the currency union comes and wages and salaries are converted even at 1:1, there will be two factors lowering the family income:

— abolition of subsidies for basic goods and services (50 billion Marks).

- growing unemployment because of the necessary structural change.

Several experts consider the low wage level to be a major factor of future competitiveness in the GDR's industry. (See Table 4).

But this competitiveness will not come true for the following reasons: (i) One of the main cost elements is

Table 3: Worker's Hourly Wages and Prices of Consumer
Goods in 1988

	GDR	FRG	FRG=100
Gross wages per hour in M/DM	8.82	23.95	36.8
Net Wages per hour in M/DM	7.35	15.99	46.0
Bread per kg	0.52	3.18	16.4
Butter per 250 g	2.50	2.15	116.3
Sugar per kg	1.55	1.91	81.2
Milk per liter	0.68	1.20	56.7
Egg	0.34	0.25	136.0
Pork per kg	8.00	10.67	75.0
Coffee per 250 g	17.50	4.47	391.5
Electricity per KWh	0.08	0.31	25.8
Color-TV	4900.00	1539.00	318.0
Washing machine	2300.00	981.00	234.5
Phone call per charge unit	0.20	0.23	87.0

Table 4: Basic Indicators of the GDR's Industry in 1988

Indicator	GDR	FRG	FRG=100
Employees in 1000	3482	7039	49
Turnover in bn. M/DM	545.0	1562.0	35
Turnover per employee in 1000 M/DM	157.0	222.0	71
Gross wages per employee in M/DM	15504.0	46495.0	33
Share of wages in prime cost in %	10.8	23.0	-
Share of material in prime cost in %	77.7	65.6	-
Enterprises total	3408	44103	8
with 10–100 employees	642	26081	2
with 101–200 employees	521	5859	9
with 201–500 employees	558	1353	41

material costs; with a 78 percent share in prime cost they
are much higher than in West Germany. (ii) If labor is
underrated, capital is overrated in the GDR's industry. A

high volume of credits is the direct result of the command system, which impedes capital formation in enterprises. 72 percent of industrial profits have been centralized by the state. The total amount of taxes, duties and royalties was 121.3 billion Marks or 22.2 percent of turnover, among them an 86.5 billion Marks deduction from profits. At present, enterprises have a debt of 260 billion Marks. A major reduction of this debt is an urgent task. The resulting deficit of the state can then be balanced by revenues from the privatization of state property, i.e., the selling of factories, land and houses. (iii) Typical for the GDR's industry are long reaction times and turnover periods and, therefore, high inventories. The relation between net product and inventories in the GDR's industry is at 1.3 and in the FRG at 2.7. But this is a direct result of a shortage economy and can be improved considerably by system transformation without immense investments. (Inventories 1989: 1987.7 billion Marks, under credit 105.1 billion Marks).

It is of course not an easy task for the industry to be suddenly confronted with world market conditions. Under the command system, state monopoly of foreign trade hindered direct contacts. Information about 110 enterprises in the electrotechnical and the machine-building industries indicates that with a conversion rate of 1:1, nearly 50 percent of the enterprises would have severe problems unless they quickly improved their cost situation.

Another serious problem is the inadequate infrastructure (transport, communications) in the GDR. But despite the complicated economic situation, one can be optimistic about system transformation in the GDR. After a period of political turbulences from August 1989 until March 1990, everybody from speculators to high-level bureaucrats made preparations for day one of the currency union. After a

period of economic turbulences, we can expect creative
destruction and rejuvenation. The key problem will be
structural change and unemployment.

Table 5 gives estimates of prospective employment
changes. In manufacturing there will be a reduction of
620,000 jobs, which is already a net figure that takes into
account a plus of one million new jobs in crafts and related
occupations. Additional capital needed could be at a level of
40 to 50 billion Marks p. a.

Table 5: Changes in Employment in the GDR (in 1000
persons)

	1988	Change
Agriculture and forestry	928	-532
Energy, water resources, mining	300	-155
Manufacturing	3182	-620
Construction	567	-33
Trade	883	-2
Transportation, communications	636	-14
Credit institutions, insurances	180	+79
Private services, free professionals	251	+799
Private households, non-profitmaking institutions	18	+297
State	2047	-746

There exist some favorable preconditions for a successful
changeover to a market economy (see Table 6):

— A qualified workforce, high discipline, order and
  organizational skills.
— A high technological level in certain branches and huge
  organizational reserves.
— The immediate use of West German knowledge in the
  reeducation process and in practice because of the
  common language.

— The social memory of a market economy, which has a long historic tradition in our country.

— The fast restoration of informal structures between West and East Germany, which were suppressed and destroyed by the old regime.

Table 6: Problems and Positive Aspects of the GDR's Economy

Positive Aspects	Problems
Qualified workforce	Meltdown of motivation Exodus
High technological level in certain branches	Decline in productivity
Well-performing agriculture	Long turnover periods
Substantial share and experience in East European markets	Unfavorable export structure
Huge organizational reserves	Underdeveloped infra-structure
Cooperation with the FRG	Delay in the economic reform
High discipline, order and organizational skills	

But we should also not forget our role as a transit country in a double sense of the word, building a bridge to the changing Eastern economies and thereby developing our traditional business contacts.

Perestroika shows the hidden traps of system transformation. Many experts agree now that a shock therapy is more advisable than a sequential strategy implemented over a long time period. In the case of Poland, the inflation process could be stopped within three months, but with a decline of 40 percent in real income (20 percent expected) and of 30 percent in production (10 percent expected).[2]

This deep recession is the most unexpected and unpleasant result of the shock therapy. What will be the most unexpected and unpleasant result of the shock therapy in the GDR? It seems to be a rapid increase of unemployment. This unemployment should allow a faster growth of productivity and output in subsequent periods.[3]

For such a higher growth rate, investment is needed. But private capital from West Germany has not yet been forthcoming. For the time being, West German investors seem to have adopted a typical wait-and-see strategy. They are waiting for two conditions: a further improvement in the institutional conditions for the use of capital and a depreciation of the existing capital stock, i.e., lower asset prices. Unfortunately, the reunification treaty will not solve these problems completely. I fear that we will loose even one of our best assets, i.e., the good business relations to our East European partners.

I see also a danger in chaotic privatization procedures that will make our people the poor of Germany. The monetary assets per person in East Germany are only a fifth as high as in West Germany (at the official 1:1 exchange rate), and the gap will become larger with the currency union (with a conversion rate of 2:1 for most monetary assets). If people then also loose their houses and land (e.g., as a result of restitution claims by West Germans), the general level of motivation for higher

---

[2] Rych [1990], pp. 13–14.

[3] See also Kornai [1990], p. 165.

productivity will be minimal, and political turbulences will return. Anyway, a deep and long trough can only be avoided if the human factor is mobilized, not demotivated, by the changes. Our chance is a process of "learning by shock," in a crash course, the lesson of the market economy which will bring down the wall that still exists in the heads of many people.

Learning by shock is a real opportunity under several conditions: (i) if the real interests of individuals are at stake, (ii) if the old system of values breaks down, and (iii) if the individuals have the freedom of choice in changing their jobs and in overcoming temporary difficulties. The first two conditions already exist in the GDR and the third one has to be developed.

Learning by shock shortens the learning period, but may also amount to a much higher effectiveness of learning. It involves a paradigmatic change that can lead to a multifaceted rearrangement of thoughts and attitudes, including psychological phenomena like inhibition (Verdrängung) and joy in the change of social roles and tasks.

The GDR has 427,000 persons in management, from supervisors to top managers. Most of them are not familiar with the paradigm and the challenges of a market economy, i.e., independence and risk-taking in a competitive environment. Many of them are clever and even creative in overcoming the obstacles of a command economy. But this is quite another job. They spent their bargaining energy in fighting the battle with central authorities, not with the market forces. Only 43,000 of them had direct market contacts with the West.

East Germany needs a complete reeducation of its managers. The capacity for requalification courses is limited. It has to be raised from 99,000 persons at present

154

to 200, 000 at least. Management education and reeducation
are becoming a major growth industry. The same will hold
for other countries in a process of system transformation.
Reeducation will contribute to overcoming the recession and
to freeing people from an obsolete and depressing system.
At the same time it should provide a sense of social
responsibility, including responsibility for future
generations.

References

INSTITUT DER DEUTSCHEN WIRTSCHAFT, *Zahlen zur
wirtschaftlichen Entwicklung in der Bundesrepublik
Deutschland*. Köln 1989.

KORNAI, Janos, Zapal'civyj pamflet po povodu
ekonomiceskogo perechoda. MNIIPU Moskva 1990.

MAIER, H., "Die Bundesrepublik auf dem Holzweg." In: *Die
Zeit*, April 13, 1990, p. 25.

RYCH, K., Pol'skaja Respublika—opyt sokovoj terapii.
MNIIPU Moskva, 1990.

STAATLICHE ZENTRALVERWALTUNG FÜR STATISTIK,
*Statistisches Jahrbuch der Deutschen Demokratischen
Republik*. Berlin 1989.

STAATSBANK DER DDR, *Jahresbericht 1989*. Berlin 1989.

DIE WIRTSCHAFT, No. 3, 1990, p. 18.

Hans Willgerodt

German Economic Integration in a European Perspective *

I. The Monetary Union between East and West Germany

The monetary union between the Germanies took effect on July 1, 1990. [1] The treaty that established it, along with a social and economic union between the countries, will become one of the most important documents in both German and European history because it avoids most of the mistakes made in many measures and proposals for European economic integration.

Beginning on July 1, 1990, the West German currency became legal tender in the GDR as well. That alone changes East Germany's economic system considerably, though not sufficiently:

— In contrast to the former East German mark, the Deutsche mark is fully convertible. That allows unlimited freedom of exchange with West Germany and the outside world. The controls on foreign exchange and the previous state monopoly of transborder monetary transactions have been eliminated entirely.

— East Germany has turned over all authority to regulate the quantity and circulation of its money to the Deutsche Bundesbank in Frankfurt, which acts independently of any government orders. At the same time, the treaty establishing a monetary union obligates the

* Abridged version of an article first published in Außenpolitik IV/1990.

[1] Press and Information Office of the West German Government [1990].

Bundesbank to assure that the currency's value remains stable.

— Except for a mere 800 million Deutsche marks, the East German government is denied free access to central bank credit.

As a result, three dangers to the GDR's economy have been eliminated: the danger of government-induced inflation (especially through deficits financed by the central bank), of floating exchange rates relative to the Deutsche mark and of currency inconvertibility. Hence there are no monetary risks to capital investment in the GDR beyond those arising from the exchange rate of the Deutsche mark. For this reason at least, the result is lower interest rates for credits extended to East Germany.

The introduction of the Deutsche mark has solved the GDR's old problem of repressed inflation, which had both a monetary and a market aspect. With regard to the former, the monetary union provides a deflationary squeeze by means of a comparatively minor currency reform. East German citizens were allowed to exchange their savings for Deutsche marks at a rate of 1 to 1 (up to 2,000 East German marks for children up to age 14; 4,000 for persons between 14 and 59; and 6,000 for persons 59 and above). Other accounts held by citizens and institutions have been converted at a rate of 2 to 1, and persons from outside the GDR have generally had to accept a rate of 3 to 1. If that fails to eliminate the monetary surplus, money can flow to West Germany to pay for imports and capital exports.

The monetary union between the Germanies goes much further than most plans for a European monetary union, including the Delors Report.[2] There is no longer much talk

_____

[2] Committee for the Study of Economic and Monetary Union [1989].

of the sort of step-by-step procedures that are envisioned in most European plans. The German monetary union was immediate and complete, resulting in unrestricted convertibility and the unreserved transfer of what has very misleadingly been called monetary sovereignty.

The GDR has opted for currency stability, even though it is imported. Insofar as it is a sovereign state, it has surrendered its monetary sovereignty. The crucial point is, to whom? It is very doubtful that East Germany would have accepted an inconvertible and politicized currency controlled by a foreign government inclined toward inflation. It wanted to transfer its monetary autonomy solely to an institution sufficiently guaranteeing the stability of money, such as the independent Deutsche Bundesbank. The treaty establishing the monetary union has strengthened the Bundesbank's independence. [3] At the same time, it has strengthened its obligation to prevent inflation. The Germanies have committed themselves to keeping the Deutsche mark stable and giving the Deutsche Bundesbank the independence and instruments it needs for that purpose.

II. Other Aspects of the Treaty between the Germanies

Although useful, the introduction of the Deutsche mark in the GDR would have been insufficient by itself. But the German negotiators avoided the mistakes of those who stressed monetary arrangements alone, without the

---

[3] Article 10 (2) states: "In order to take advantage of the currency union, the value of the currency in the German Democratic Republic must be stable; by the same token, the stability of the currency in the Federal Republic of Germany must be ensured."

additional measures necessary to ensure the smooth functioning of a monetary union.[4] After much discussion within the EC, it is clear that a monetary union cannot work without the free movement of goods and labor, free capital transactions and payments, free markets and prices. The treaty establishing a monetary, social and economic union between the Germanies prescribes a social market economy marked by private property, effective competition, freely determined prices and, as a rule, the free movement of labor, goods and services. Public property is allowed so long as there is no discrimination against private property. Environmental protection, a labor market compatible with the new economic order and a comprehensive social security system are further aspects of the treaty. The Germanies committed themselves to a free, democratic, federal, constitutional system, to freedom of contract, business, profession, residence, movement, to form associations and, last but not least, private ownership of land and the means of production.

The endless debate within the EC on harmonizing the tax and social security systems and regulations for business and technology was not repeated between the Germanies. Instead, the crucial elements of the West German legal system were simply extended to the GDR. Unfortunately, that included some of West Germany's more irrational laws, such as the one requiring self-employed craftsmen to be certified masters of their trade, and regulations and quotas limiting competition on the long-distance trucking of freight. East Germany's agricultural regulations, protectionist in nature, are even more irrational than the

---

[4] For a critique of the Werner Plan as well as of other plans submitted before 1970, see Willgerodt et al. [1972].

EC's. So the two German markets for agricultural products have not merged to a large extent.

The GDR has adopted West Germany's foreign trade system for the most part, including the rules established by the EC. That means breaking with the Council of Mutual Economic Assistance (COMECON, CMEA), which is in the process of dissolving anyway. Ways will have to be found to continue trade with COMECON members. The GDR will even try to expand this trade, capitalizing on its advantages vis-à-vis Eastern Europe: a better knowledge of the languages and economic conditions and established economic ties.

At first, many West German economists, myself included,[5] thought it was possible to establish a market economy in the GDR without a monetary union. In that case, the East German currency would have had to be stabilized, made convertible and linked to the outside world by flexible exchange rates. After a period of adaptation and restructuring, the exchange rate could have been fixed to the Deutsche mark and a common German currency could have been introduced. Some experts preferred to fix the exchange rate immediately, defending it, if necessary, by imposing controls that could have been gradually removed.[6] Others preferred floating exchange rates and decontrolling foreign exchange transactions step by step.

All of these proposals proved to be unfeasible, not only for political but also for economic reasons:

— Even with a separate currency, East Germans could have compared their real wages with those paid out in West

---

[5] Willgerodt [1990].

[6] See, for instance, Engels et al. [1990].

Germany; hence hoping to stop emigration to the Federal Republic by means of a floating exchange rate was unrealistic.

— The opening of the GDR's western border made floating exchange rates a less useful option in helping East Germany adapt production to free-market conditions than would otherwise have been the case. With the free movement of labor and free trade with the West, real prices would have extended from West Germany into the GDR to such a degree that changes in the exchange rate would have determined East German real incomes to nearly the same extent as equivalent changes in nominal prices and nominal incomes will in the currency union. Floating exchange rates would not have created enough of an illusion of price and wage stability to make the problem of unemployment and unrealistic wages solvable by Keynesian inflationary measures.

— It is doubtful whether floating exchange rates would have effected the necessary changes in the price *structure*. Convertibility and free trade with West Germany would inevitably have led to the West German price structure for tradable goods, regardless of the exchange rate. The number of goods traded between the Germanies would have risen sharply and the East German price system would have come to mirror that of the West. Nor would a floating exchange rate have had any advantages as far as nontradable goods are concerned. Many of them have prices that are artificially low, and in the currency union most of them are bound to rise. Rents, fares, land prices and the like must be raised to free-market levels to ensure the economic use of capital and land neglected for more than 50 years. Although political considerations prevent raising these prices immediately, the introduction of the hard Deutsche mark will at least increase the real value of the prices that are being paid. Had the GDR retained its currency, the result could have been inflation and a more distorted price structure caused by lowering the real value of controlled prices for the nontradables whose prices would have remained fixed by the government.

Given the fact that border controls have ceased, the immediate extension of West Germany's price structure to the GDR via the currency union has undermined all plans to protect the East German economy by the continued control of foreign exchange, autonomous tariffs, taxes and quotas.

In sum, introducing the Deutsche mark into the GDR is much more than simply a change of currency. It is a lever with which to change the economic and political system in the GDR and switch to a market economy. Adopting the West German price system gives East German companies a reliable basis for their economic calculations, which would have been more difficult under flexible exchange rates. Economic policy has a psychological as well as a technical aspect. The Deutsche mark has an international reputation whose influence on economic decisions is incalculable but definitely positive. That applies primarily to investment in East Germany. The treaty between the Germanies fulfills what Wilhelm Röpke declared in 1950 to be the minimum requirements for a functioning market economy. In his report to the West German government on its economic policy, he cited free trade, unrestricted international monetary transactions and a free capital market.[7] In all three areas, East Germany now accepts West German rules.

There is, however, one genuinely difficult problem. Up to 1945, private property in Germany—including ownership of the means of production—was allowed by law but

---

[7] Röpke [1950], p. 23.

restricted in fact because proprietors were subject to orders issued by the government's economic planners. The West German reform of 1948 gave proprietors the right to use their property as they saw fit. In East Germany, meanwhile, the Communists virtually eliminated private ownership of the means of production, replacing it with state ownership and centralized cooperatives. Without private ownership of the means of production, decentralized production sufficient for the needs of a market economy is impossible, which militates against a functioning market economy. For this reason, the treaty between the Germanies calls for large-scale denationalization, with state-owned companies first being legally converted into private companies, shares in which are then sold to the public. At the same time, there is a painful restructuring process in which companies adapt to free market conditions. Bankrupt companies will be liquidated. All of this will take time, but the introduction of a free market and the Deutsche mark could not wait. On the contrary, without a free market there would have been no guidelines for appropriate restructuring measures and for realistic prices for shares in the new companies. So the market had to come first.

Accounts and balances of East German businesses now have to be calculated in Deutsche marks and at the new market values. In many cases that means a loss of assets that prove to be useless and have to be written off. The treaty cuts the credit obligations of East German companies by 50 percent. At the same time, however, interest rates for old and new credits may rise.

That leads to further problems. Under the Communists, many East German companies had to turn a portion of their depreciation amounts over to the state, i. e., they could not even keep enough funds to replace worn out capital goods. Instead, they had to rely on credits from the state banking system. After the reform, businesses must still repay those old debts, which in many cases do not reflect the past and potential profitability of their capital. It would have been better to forgive the old debt completely instead of solving the problem case by case. Moreover, financing will be handled by the newly privatized state bank, whose staff is largely made up of holdovers from the old era with little knowledge of credit transactions in a market economy. Thus the treaty allows the more profitable businesses, and those with the highest growth potential, to be squeezed because they are the only ones able to service the old debt. Their development will be inhibited to some extent because profits that could otherwise be used for expansion, and payments on the interest and principal of their debts, may be used to subsidize unprofitable companies for political or social reasons.

The argument that writing off all the old debts would result in financial losses for the state bank is unfounded. The state body in charge of restructuring and denationalizing the companies could sell them off at a higher price once the debts are nullified. The higher price could be used in turn to raise payments on the state bank. The bank should not be allowed to drive viable companies into bankruptcy by insisting on repayment of old debts regardless of the company's potential. The treaty's Article 14 provides for alterations to restructuring procedures, so there is some hope that mismanagement of the debt problem can be averted.

III. A New Germany in a New Europe

The prospect of a united Germany is frightening for many countries and for some Germans as well, many of them socialists.[8] The term "socialism" loses all precision if it is not defined as central economic and social planning. Quite a few socialists, Germans among them, define it that way—either directly or indirectly by rejecting the basic principles of a market economy.[9] If a united Germany were socialist by this definition, fear would indeed be justified because the consequence would either be the breakup of the free-market system in Europe or, if a socialist Germany sought to dominate Europe and export its centrally administered system to its neighbors, the breakup of the international order. If those German socialists opposing reunification thought logically, something they unfortunately rarely do, they would have to ascribe their fears to their own socialist creed, which makes them see the German economy as a centrally controlled instrument of power politics.

Non-socialists who are against a single Germany, and are aware that reunification means the extension of West Germany's market economy and liberal democratic form of government onto former socialist territory, are guilty of logical inconsistencies. A liberal order and market economy eliminate the economic incentive for territorial gains, making national borders less relevant from an economic standpoint. Why should a German free-trade area larger than the Federal Republic become more aggressive? The only possible reason would arise from political and militaristic ambitions independent of, and even conflicting with, the country's economic interests. But that is a moot point because the

---

[8] See, among others, Habermas [1990]; Grass [1990].

[9] On the problems democratic socialism has in bridging the gap between central planning and liberal democracy, see Willgerodt [1985].

German army is fully integrated into NATO and the domestic political system—with all the checks and balances of decentralized government—does not permit hostile acts against other countries. The German government, by virtue of its constitution, does not have the power that the highly centralized governments of Great Britain, France and Italy do. There is no absolute "sovereignty" held by a parliament or some other central body; rather, there is a division of authority. "Sovereignty" is no longer a "rocher de bronze," as it was in the days of Prussian King Friedrich Wilhelm I. The Federal Republic's Basic Law prevents comprehensive economic planning by the state. Only socialists would want to introduce such planning, which would allow renewed German aggressiveness.

Most German socialists are not aware of this connection and would deny it were they confronted with it. To be sure, they are not aggressively inclined themselves, at least not toward other countries. But their cherished central planning is intrinsically aggressive in nature. It is therefore important that the West German constitution does not allow such a system to be established. Once the GDR joins the Federal Republic on the basis of Article 23 of the West German Basic Law, aggressiveness stemming from a centrally administered economy is ruled out. The West German constitutional principle of decentralized government is immutable, as is the catalogue of basic civil rights. The West German constitutional court has proved to be one of the system's most effective institutions in resisting illegal extensions of government power. Hence the legal and political system of the Federal Republic is comparatively foolproof.

If other European countries are interested in avoiding a recurrence of German power politics, they should make sure that European economic policy does not allow far-reaching government intervention and planning. Centralized regulations by European institutions aimed at establishing a centralized European "nation" are apt to provoke a controversy over which country will have the most influence in the European union. In that case, a united Germany would have a better chance of imposing its will on others than before. Moreover, if centralized European interventionism were adopted, the Germans would naturally seek to have their own way. When British Prime Minister Margaret Thatcher and her political friends express their uneasiness about German unification, they should realize that Germany's current economic and political order automatically blocks any conceivable desires to dominate other countries. The British position is inconsistent. It emphasises the predominance of national sovereignty and rejects supranational obligations binding on the British Parliament. [10] It would be interesting to know whether this absolute freedom of decision is seen as applying to Germany as well, which could then leave the EC if its legislature so decided.

The West German attitude is different. The Federal Republic's constitution does not give unlimited power to the German parliament, not to speak of the federal chancellor. The principle of divided authority is also followed in Germany's international relations. Article 24 of the Basic Law of the Federal Republic provides for the partial transfer of national sovereignty to supranational institutions such as those of the EC. Unfortunately, views of such a transfer are varied. Germans who still think in terms of Great Prussian centralism would be glad to recentralize the German Länder (i.e., states). They see Europe as a quasi-

---

[10] See Sked [1990].

national superstate in which German nationhood would be largely lost. If they advocate a European free market at all, they term it a "Binnenmarkt" (i.e., internal market) and give little heed to discrimination against the outside world, i.e., they think in terms of a closed, highly centralized system. But German history is not confined to Prussian-style centralism, of course. There was also the Holy Roman Empire and the German Confederation, for example. Europeans distrustful of the Germans should work toward a united Europe that is not another superpower or centrally administered "fortress" with central economic planning, but an internationally open, constitutional entity sufficiently strong to cope with irrational developments in its member states.

References

COMMITTEE FOR THE STUDY OF ECONOMIC AND MONETARY UNION, *Report on Economic and Monetary Union in the European Community*. Brussels, April 17, 1989.

ENGELS, Wolfram, Walter HAMM, Otmar ISSING, Wernhard MÖSCHEL, and Olaf SIEVERT (KRONBERGER KREIS), *Soziale Marktwirtschaft in der DDR. Währungsordnung und Investitionsbedingungen*. Bad Homburg, January 1990.

GRASS, Günther, *Deutscher Lastenausgleich. Wider das dumpfe Einheitsgebot. Reden und Gespräche*. Frankfurt am Main 1990.

HABERMAS, Jürgen, *Die nachholende Revolution*. Frankfurt am Main 1990.

PRESS AND INFORMATION OFFICE OF THE WEST GERMAN GOVERNMENT, *Bulletin*, No. 63, 1990, p. 517-544.

RÖPKE, Wilhelm, *Ist die deutsche Wirtschaftspolitik richtig? Analyse und Kritik*. Stuttgart 1950.

SKED, Alan, A Proposal for European Union, The Bruges Group, Occasional Paper 9, London, May 1990.

WILLGERODT, Hans, Alexander DOMSCH, Rolf HASSE, and Volker MERX, *Wege und Irrwege zur europäischen Währungsunion*. Freiburg im Breisgau 1972.

WILLGERODT, Hans, "Thesen zum "demokratischen Sozialismus"." In: Anton RAUSCHER (ed.), *Selbstinteresse und Gemeinwohl*. Berlin 1985, pp. 229-277.

——, "Wirtschaftsordnung für ein anderes Deutschland— Wege aus der Krise der DDR." In: *Zeitschrift für Wirtschaftspolitik*, Vol. 39, 1990, pp. 103-169.

List of Contributors

Professor Tamás Bauer
    Professor of Economics at the Institute of Economics in Budapest, Hungary, and the Johann Wolfgang Goethe-Universität in Frankfurt am Main.

Professor Dr. Drs. h. c. Herbert Giersch
    Professor of Economics (emeritus), former President of the Institut für Weltwirtschaft, Kiel.

Professor Dr. sc. Heinz-Dieter Haustein
    Professor of Economics at the Hochschule für Ökonomie in Berlin, GDR.

Dr. Václav Klaus
    Minister of Finance of Czechoslovakia.

Karol Lutkowski
    Advisor to the Minister of Finance of Poland.

Holger Schmieding
    Research Economist at the Institut für Weltwirtschaft in Kiel.

Professor Dr. Hans Willgerodt
    Professor of Economics (emeritus) at the Universität Köln.

Professor Jan Winiecki, Ph. D.
    Professor of Economics at the Institute for Labour Research in Warsaw.

Dr. Vladimir Zuev
    Research Economist at the Institute of World Economy and International Relations in Moscow.